My Son's Siblings

A Queer Parent's Memoir on the Joys, Grief, and Ethics of Donor Conception

Eli Ramos

Dedicated to my family.

CONTENTS

CHAPTER ONE

LIVING IN THE LIMINAL

This is a story about family—the kind you build, the kind you inherit, and the kind you find unexpectedly. It's also about navigating life when no blueprint exists, and when you have to invent language as you go. It's about identity, truth-telling and making peace with uncertainty.

My life has been an endless journey through liminal spaces. I've never done what I was "supposed" to do, or what people expected of me. Take four-year-old me, for example. While other little girls asked for pigtails or bows, I was inspired by the grungy, tattooed punks surrounding our illegal, roach-infested sublet apartment. Such was the West Village of New York City in the 90s.

I begged my parents for a mohawk (specifically one I would dye purple, green and pink) because I wanted to be like them—cool and different. Proudly unique. They said no, shocker, but that I *could* shave my head (probably assuming I'd back out). Instead, I walked into my dad's surprisingly large barbershop in a basement in Astor Place, head held high, and watched my curly locks fall to the ground. I rocked that buzz cut. I *loved* when people mistook me for a boy or gave me confused looks. I lost count of how many times I heard, "Girls can't have short hair." Then, what am I? From an early age, I knew I'd rather be authentic than fit in.

With many of my identities, including my queerness, I've lived my life without a map to go by. Gay marriage became legal in my home state when I was a junior in college, and the landmark 2015 Supreme Court case Obergefell v. Hodges[i] made marriage equality the standard nationwide when I was in my early twenties. I am a queer American with rights unlike any before me. I have a new kind of life to live, one that hasn't been modeled for me. And now, as a parent, I'm stepping into new territory again, creating my own map, and maybe, if I'm lucky, becoming a model for others who will follow.

Coming out as queer when I was 20 wasn't a huge shock to me. After my buzz-cut story it's probably not a shock to you, either. In my adolescent years, while I was attracted to women, I never spoke about it to anyone. It wasn't "normal," and I knew it. Not because anyone explicitly told me but because of everything around me—what I saw on TV, in books, in the people I met, and not to mention the church services my family attended (anyone else up for eternal damnation?). The world seemed to revolve around straight, cis, "normal" people. Any queer (or even more rare, transgender) representation that existed was either a punchline or something to be ashamed of. I was eventually bullied for my short hair, so I grew it out. But queerness? If I was queer, it wasn't something I could hide. It wasn't something I could disguise or change like a haircut. So, it stayed unexplored, shrouded in shame, for far too many years.

Another contributing factor to my unexplored queerness was my relationship with my high school/early college boyfriend. It's the kind of first love you dream of where the cute guy a grade above you not only sees you but reciprocates your crush. We fell deeply in love and spent the next few years in a kind, fulfilling relationship.

When I first came out (not with labels but by saying,

"I'm dating Kate now"), I wondered if my queerness somehow invalidated my relationship with him. In the lesbian community, there's a term: *gold-star lesbian*. It refers to someone who has never been with a man. Needless to say, that kind of rhetoric is dismissive and harmful.

Over time, I've embraced the words queer and pansexual, which are terms that allow more room for complexity. They let me look back on the relationship for what it was: wonderful. It was my first love, my first relationship, and one that I look back on with incredible fondness.

When I began my next romantic relationship at 20, I fell head over heels for the second time in my life, but this time, it was for a woman. I immediately wondered how I had ever questioned whether it was okay. Not only was it okay, but it was also beautiful! I'd revived a piece of my confident, expectation-shirking younger self and started exploring a world that felt both unfamiliar and exciting. I had graduated from church (*hallelujah*) to church (*yes, gawd*), and breaking free of some of the conventions that had ruled my life felt like breathing fresh air for the first time.

This first "coming out," though, was a process. I wasn't sure what my future might look like anymore. I remember telling Kate that I still pictured myself ending up with a man because I probably wanted to have kids (I can hear my wife's cackle as I type this). At the time, I couldn't yet imagine a queer version of parenthood that felt real or attainable. The only models I had were straight couples with biological (or transracially adopted) kids, and everything else felt like a fantasy. Back then, "queer parent" felt mostly like an oxymoron, or at least an exception to the rule. But eventually, as I kept choosing authenticity over expectation, the future I couldn't picture started to come into view.

The person I was back then would probably keel over if they saw the life I've built now. Not only do I have a wife I love dearly, Melissa, but we share a beautiful child together (despite neither of us having penises!). We conceived our son Riley using a sperm donor from a cryobank. At one point we had considered asking a friend to be our donor, but we were nervous about the potential complications—like whether his family might want to be more involved than we were comfortable with, or whether it would create fractures in our friendship. Choosing a donor through a cryobank felt like the simplest way to have the kind of family we imagined: just the two of us and our kid.

If I were starting my family-building journey today, knowing what I know now, I might have made a different choice. However, I wouldn't go back and change a thing. My son is the best human I know. That said, I owe him my deepest reflection, ongoing self-awareness, and the constant work of showing up—for him, and for the complexities shaped by the decisions Melissa and I have made, like which cryobank we would use or who our sperm donor would be.

Choosing a donor is a weird experience. You're sitting at your laptop, looking through profiles on a screen, each with varying amounts of information about the person they represent. Imagine scrolling through Tinder but not to meet someone or fall in love. You're choosing someone to help you make a child—and it's someone you'll probably never actually meet or know.

One of the first decisions we made was about the level of anonymity we were comfortable with. We knew we wanted someone classified as non-anonymous, meaning the donor agrees to have his contact information shared with any offspring when they turn eighteen. We couldn't imagine what it might feel like for our future kid to *never* have access to that information.

So, that became our main filter alongside health history and *vibe*. You know, that part you can't really explain but you just feel.

After narrowing the options to about twenty "maybes," Melissa and I each dove deeper into the profiles. We separately ranked our top five to help guide our next conversation. As it turned out, we didn't need a long discussion—we had both chosen the same clear favorite: Donor 2XC89. Tears fell as we made this momentous (and expensive) decision. We had chosen our donor, and we placed our order.

Melissa became pregnant via intrauterine insemination at a fertility clinic on our fifth vial of sperm. That pregnancy stuck, and our beautiful son Riley was born nine months later. While I felt extremely prepared for infant care—as someone who practically grew up in their family's daycare and worked there for years as an adult—I had no idea how unprepared I was to confront the realities of what my son's life might be like as a donor-conceived person.

We had been so focused on getting him here that we hadn't looked far past that. Beyond choosing the most open cryobank donor we could find the deeper questions didn't even come up. And when he arrived, we found ourselves in another liminal space, once again, without any guidelines. We weren't a traditional family, and there was no script for how to navigate this journey.

Although I was unprepared in terms of knowledge and language, what I didn't realize then was that I was well-equipped to tackle this deeply emotional and complex terrain. Because at its core, this is a journey of identity, and if I've learned anything from my own experiences, it's that identity is never fixed. It evolves, shifts, and expands in ways that words fail to describe. I've learned this through my own journey as a queer, agnostic, multiracial, nonbinary person, and I see it unfolding in real time with Riley. His identity isn't static. As he grows, his understanding of himself, his family, and his origins will keep shifting. We know we'll have to try on language, explore stories, and shape a narrative of our family that feels true to us and true to him.

If you've ever found yourself living between definitions, making it up as you go, this is for you.

CHAPTER TWO

THE JOURNEY TO (QUEER) PARENTHOOD

If I'm being truly honest with myself, I have always had a deep desire to be a parent. You would find me most days after school in the infant room of my parents' daycare, choosing to spend my free time with the youngest children in our care.

When I was first exploring my queerness in 2010, my desire to be a parent faded slightly. Maybe it was self-protective—I couldn't picture having a child as a queer person. At the time, gay marriage was only legal in five states. In chronological order, they were: Massachusetts, Connecticut, Iowa, Vermont and New Hampshire. My home state of New York would take another year before joining the list. Queer parenthood in this landscape felt difficult, expensive, and discriminatory—generally out of reach. I didn't even know who I'd end up with, anyway. There was so much unknown, and having kids wasn't top-of-mind when I couldn't yet imagine a future partner, let alone a family.

And then, Melissa entered my life—a vibrant, gorgeous, caring, intelligent, all-around incredible woman. We, ironically, met in person while working for a dating app. We were part of a team that volunteered their time to put on events for single queer people to meet in real life, without having to swipe and read profiles. We were creating safe spaces for people to meet and fall in love. Including ourselves, apparently.

I had a crush on her from the very first meeting. We were eight queers sitting at a table in a Hell's Kitchen restaurant, all meeting for the first time except for the pair that were already a couple. There was one person, a literal comedian, sitting between Melissa and me over dinner. I watched Melissa throw her head back with laughter, and I was instantly smitten. I even texted my cousin, excited about the cute single girl I'd just met. After dinner, we went out dancing and I tried my damnedest to keep Melissa out, despite the fact that we both had to be at our paying jobs early the next day.

We were friends harboring secret crushes for a few months, but once we started dating, we admitted we were in love within three weeks (cue obligatory "lesbians move so fast they bring a U-Haul on the second date" joke). Someone recently asked us, "Who made the first move?" The truth is: alcohol. Our feelings for one another grew over the first few months of our friendship, but we were each harboring our own bitter flavors of self-doubt. Before our very first meeting, Melissa had promised herself she wouldn't hook up with anyone on the team because she really wanted queer friends. On my end, I hadn't dated anyone since coming out as nonbinary and had a lot of questions about what romantic relationships might look like for me now. But one night at the bar, liquid courage aboard, we finally let ourselves act on our feelings. And we never looked back.

The following year, we moved into our little basement apartment, and the year after that, we got engaged. We knew it would be a long engagement. Weddings are expensive, after all. Neither of us come from financial privilege, and that matters, because having a child the way we did requires a certain level of access and resources. Back then, the biggest obstacle we foresaw to becoming parents was money. But thanks to pre-wedding financial gifts from my parents and a wedding venue offer from a family friend, we were able to pay off student debt, plan a small

COVID-era wedding, and even begin to imagine a future as parents. To boot, my job at our family's daycare meant childcare, a major obstacle for most prospective parents, would be free. Suddenly, having a family started to feel like a real possibility.

Everything I hadn't even let myself dream of was falling into place.

The year was 2020, and now we had plenty to do during COVID quarantine: plan our wedding and plan our family. We started talking about what our dream family might look like. That's when it started to feel real. We were taking concrete steps toward a life I hadn't believed was possible for people like us.

After deciding against asking a friend to be our sperm donor, we began researching other options. We knew a couple who had built their family through RIVF—Reciprocal In Vitro Fertilization—where one partner's eggs are fertilized with donor sperm, and the other partner carries the pregnancy. It struck us as an incredibly beautiful way for two partners with uteruses to be physically and emotionally involved in creating a family.

We already knew, though, that IVF was out of our price range and started looking into other options. We had both grown up as one of three siblings, and we wanted our future children to have at least one sibling to grow up with. After looking into various options, we decided that our ideal scenario would be that we each carry one pregnancy using the same sperm donor. It felt like a way for our family, and our children, to reflect both of us while having a common factor.

Next, we started looking into cryobanks. We knew already that we didn't want to use one of the less regulated pathways to finding a sperm donor like Facebook groups. We didn't even know much about them at the time. We liked the feeling that cryobanks had a variety of processes for screening donors, setting family limits, and providing some background information. It felt more structured, and therefore, safer.

There were a few cryobanks that were explicitly welcoming to queer families, which was the first thing we looked for. One stood out to us. Maybe it was just the layout of the website, or maybe it was something as subconscious as the color scheme, but it felt easier to navigate and more transparent somehow. It felt like we could get to know the donors as people, not just random strings of letters and numbers. So, we chose it.

And then came the harder part: choosing a donor.

At the time, it felt lighthearted, fun, even, to imagine our future child and scroll through profiles together. We sat on the couch, scrolling through the page and saying, "Wait, click that one!" We joked about whose hair color the baby might inherit, whose height, whose quirks—partially to distract ourselves from how odd it felt. We were making a deeply intimate choice in a highly impersonal way. It was equal parts fun and weird. It's so incredible and exciting to imagine becoming a parent and holding your child for the first time but so clinical choosing someone to help fulfill that dream based on a checklist, instead of because you love them. Back then, although it felt odd, we didn't think to question the system we were participating in.

Looking back now, I see this part quite differently. I've since learned how deeply rooted the fertility industry is in systems of exclusion and eugenics. Clinicians and cryobanks historically (and still today) filter, prioritize, and market certain kinds of bodies and identities over others. It's inescapable. Even as we made the best choices we could with the information we had, I now know that we were operating inside a deeply flawed and unjust system.

In those early moments though, we were just two people dreaming of a family, trying to create a future.

One of the first things we realized was that we each imagined our donor looking like the other (and we look nothing alike). It spoke to that quiet sadness we both carried that we couldn't create a child between the two of us. There is often grief woven into the process of fertility treatment. For straight, cisgender couples, that grief might come from the heartbreak of infertility, the loss of assumed virility, or the unexpected reality of not sharing a genetic link with their future child. For many queer couples like us, it's a different kind of ache: the sadness of knowing *from the outset* that we won't be able to see both of us, at least not genetically, in our child. It's the reminder that we won't resemble the families we come from, or the majority of the families we see around us. Our path to parenthood is harder, more expensive, more scrutinized, less common, and less supported than others.

We briefly considered the idea of choosing a donor who looked like me for the pregnancy Melissa would carry, and one who looked like her for the one I would carry, but that idea never had legs for us. What mattered most to us ended up not being resemblance but emotional connection to the donor. We cared more about creating a biological bond between our future children than whether they looked like us. In the end, we found that we didn't care much about physical features at all.

As we went through profiles together, we filtered first for donors who agree to allow future contact once a child turns 18 and soon realized there was something else that we cared about. We wanted to see a photo (an option some cryobanks make you pay for). A description, no matter how detailed, didn't feel like enough. It felt strange enough to be building a family with a stranger; not even knowing what that person looked like felt unimaginable. We wanted to get a sense of that vibe you can only feel when you see someone's face.

Together, we scrolled through profiles, mixing excitement with reflection. Did height matter to us? Level of education? Occupation? There was so much information, but how much we cared about each piece varied wildly. We kept reminding ourselves to stay open-minded and eventually crafted a list of around 20 "favorites," or profiles we wanted to return to and consider more deeply.

Then, we decided to take time individually with the profiles. It had been helpful to look together, but sharing a screen made it hard to read deeply or sit with our own thoughts and feelings. We agreed to each create a personal "top five" based on the favorites list to guide our next conversation: Who was standing out to us? Why? We hoped we'd have at least one common donor in our individual top-five lists, or that it would guide our next conversation and help us narrow down the field.

I remember the visceral feeling when I dove into the profile of the person who would become my top donor. At first, I almost didn't even want him on our favorites list because he is mixed-race. I'm part Asian, and so is he, but his Asian ancestry came from a different country than my own. When we first clicked on his profile, I asked Melissa if it was ethical to choose him as a donor, knowing this. We talked about it briefly, but this was at the stage where we kept reminding each other to keep an open mind, or we'd have no list at all. We knew we'd have time to dig into that question later if it still applied. And now, it was time to answer that question.

It's complicated. I would never have chosen a donor who was fully of a different race from us, but what about partially? How "diluted" did that ancestry have to be before it felt acceptable? I am part Filipino, and it has been a huge piece of my identity. I grew up loving my *Pinoy Pamilya*. My lolo is the grandparent I was always closest with growing up. I have a tiny patch on my left forearm that is slightly darker than the rest of my body. I've always thought of it as a little piece of lolo, who had gorgeous brown skin. I cherish it so much that when I started getting tattoos, dreaming of a sleeve one day, I decided on inking my right arm so that my lolo patch would remain untouched.

To add to my love of my lolo's culture, my neighborhood was so full of fellow Filipinos that they sang in Tagalog at our Sunday church services. It was a real and meaningful part of my life. Yet, I always carried the feeling that I wasn't Asian enough. I was mostly white, and looked mostly white, especially compared to my Asian peers. I didn't speak Tagalog. I didn't face the same experiences they did. I often felt like an outsider trying to claim something that didn't fully belong to me.

To make things even more complicated, my last name, Ramos, also from my lolo, led most people to assume I was from a Spanish-speaking country. I lost count of how many times someone started speaking to me in Spanish, confused when I couldn't keep up. For me, it has always felt like my name told a story about me that wasn't wrong exactly, but also wasn't quite right. Ramos is a Spanish name, a remnant of the centuries Spain spent colonizing the Philippines. That colonization shaped everything from the language to the religion to the surnames, but it didn't erase the deep and distinct cultures that existed long before. Having a Spanish last name meant people often made assumptions that didn't match my family's real history.

My identity became something layered, complicated, neither fully here nor there. As I've mentioned already, identity always felt like something I was both reaching for and being miscast in. Always too much in some ways, and not enough in others. My future children would inherit the confusion that comes with my last name but potentially none of the heritage from which it originates.

In the end, the part of me that feels the most Filipino isn't something you can see. It's not in the shape of my eyes or the color of my skin. It's in the intangibles: the deep sense of joy, the generosity, the way family always comes first. Those were the things my Filipino side gave me; the parts that shaped my heart more than any visible trait ever could.

I remember another profound moment when the development of my queer identity collided with my Filipino heritage. It was when I first learned about the deep, pre-colonial history of gender fluidity and homosexuality in Filipino culture (as with many indigenous cultures around the world). These identities weren't just accepted; they were commonplace, free of shame, and in some cases, even held positions of spiritual authority as *Babaylan* (shaman). While I, as a nonbinary person, typically strive for tolerance, my nonbinary ancestors were more than accepted; they were revered. Of course, colonization changed all that. Centuries of imposed Western beliefs and values stripped much of that acceptance away, leaving behind the same discriminatory practices and attitudes that still persist in the Philippines (and in much of the world) today. But I felt connected to this pre-colonial history. It was something I could claim as part of who I was, and I felt it on a cellular level.

So, when thinking about this donor, all of these old, tangled feelings came up again. How could I knowingly choose a donor whose ancestry wasn't ours to share? Would it be fair to raise a child with a background we didn't fully represent? Would my child miss out on opportunities to connect with their heritage? Would they feel that same in-between feeling I'd grown up carrying?

There's no neat answer. There never is.

And yet, there was so much about this donor that drew

me in. The vibes were immaculate. He seemed family-oriented, genuine, and kind. He loved animals, played sports and instruments, and just felt, in the simplest terms, like someone we would want to be friends with in real life.

Ultimately, I decided his race and ethnicity were not a limiting factor for me. It was part of the story, not the entirety. I imagined speaking openly with our child about their full heritage, from all sides, and supporting whatever curiosity or identity-building came from it. I hoped that would be enough. I still do.

I knew Melissa had already made her list and was ready for the donor discussion, but I was dragging my feet. Somehow, deep down, I knew he was her favorite, too. I took a risk and printed out his picture. I folded it up neatly, and placed it on the coffee table with a note that I had finished my list and that, once unfolded, the paper would reveal my favorite. When Melissa got home from working late that night, she opened it immediately.

She startled me awake, sobbing: "He's my number one, too."

It wasn't the same as having a child together, but choosing him, separately and then together, felt like proof that when it came to parenthood we were already on the same page in the ways that mattered most.

This donor had one small asterisk. He was a carrier for a genetic condition. After reading the fine print, and knowing we would be able to change donors if one of us was found to also be a carrier, we were ready to take the next step. But there were so many more questions: How many vials should we buy? What kind of vials? What methods of conception will we try?

It was a month before our wedding, but we had 100% confidence in where we wanted our lives to go. We knew we were ready to make this decision, even if we weren't ready to figure out logistics or start trying immediately. We wanted to have all the pieces in place to start trying to have a child as soon as we decided we were ready.

Knowing we wanted two kids, and reading that (on average) four vials are needed for a successful pregnancy via our primary method, IUI (intrauterine insemination), we decided we would purchase eight vials. We got a few ICI (intracervical insemination) vials as well because we wanted to see what we could accomplish on our own before trying at a clinic. We assumed vial availability went relatively quickly, so we wanted to get all the vials we might need right away rather than buy a few now and risk a lack of availability in the future. It was a huge cost for us. Vials were around $1,000 apiece, but we had just enough money to make it work and enough faith in our dream to take the leap.

We placed the call, anxiously gave our credit card number over the phone, and bought our vials. It felt way too simple for such a momentous expense. It was, to date, the single biggest purchase of either of our lives.

Our next major decision ended up being an easy one: who would carry first? Melissa is a little older, and in her words, "If I had to watch you do it first, there's no way in hell I'd go through with it." I burst out laughing because I knew she was absolutely right. It's classic Melissa logic, and with that one line the decision was made. Melissa would carry first.

Sometimes people are surprised to hear that I'm open to carrying a pregnancy. My masculine presentation mixed with pregnancy seems to short-circuit people's brains. It brings me back to being the little kid with a buzz cut, answering for the hundredth time why a little boy would want to wear earrings. It's always been a strange dichotomy. I'm proud of who I am, but it's exhausting to constantly explain myself. People tend to view pregnancy as inherently feminine, so they're confused that someone who has rejected being labeled a woman would still want to experience it.

I sometimes wonder if I ever had a "ring of keys" moment like Alison Bechdel recounts in her iconic graphic novel *Fun Home*. It describes a single flash of recognition, when something outside of you suddenly reflects something true inside. I try to remember if I ever had my own "ring of keys" moment, but when I think about it, mine wasn't a particular moment, it was a feeling.

The community I grew up in was full of people living visibly and unapologetically: punks with mohawks, piercings and tattoos; people in drag; neighbors speaking a dozen different languages and sharing their cultures in everyday ways. I was surrounded by authenticity, even if I didn't have the tools or language yet to express my own.

Children don't have as many outlets for self-expression, but as I explained earlier, I made do. I wore my buzz cut like a badge of honor for five whole years. I loved the shocked looks I received from strangers, catching them off guard in the best way. Reflecting on it now, I realize I've always been drawn to moments that pull back the curtain and expand what's possible.

Today, there's still some cognitive dissonance between my body and my identity. I've never taken testosterone or had gender-affirming surgery. It's partially because I'm already taking thyroid hormone replacements daily and don't want to add more to the mix. But mostly it's because, for me, living authentically has meant accepting the body I have, even if it doesn't always align with how I feel inside. If this body is capable of carrying a pregnancy, I think that's pretty damn cool—and something I'd be lucky to experience if I get the chance. That said, I wouldn't feel as safe as a masculine presenting pregnant person as I felt as a child with a unique haircut. That's another bridge I'll cross if I am lucky enough to get to it.

The pieces were falling into place, and a plan was forming. Three months after our wedding, we were ready for our first insemination attempt at home, via Intracervical Insemination (known familiarly as the "turkey baster method").

After securing the paperwork needed to inseminate at home, which turned out to be quite a tricky feat only made possible with the help of a family friend/physician, we began tracking ovulation and learning all we could to maximize our chances. We didn't realize at the time just how low the odds of success were for at home ICI with frozen sperm. I'm not sure if we were oblivious or naïvely idealistic, but we called the cryobank to set up our delivery.

The vials are shipped in a container that keeps them frozen for an extended period of time which is extremely convenient when you don't have a consistent cycle. We thought we had the timing of Melissa's ovulation right, and we went for it.

What a strange, surreal experience.

We opened the cryopreservation tank and pulled out the vial of sperm. It was no bigger than a medium paper clip, and barely half full. This tiny, absurdly expensive vial held all our hopes and dreams inside.

We let it thaw, doing our best to ignore the awkwardness in the air. When you imagine conceiving a child with your partner, you imagine something romantic, intimate and beautiful. We tried our best. I cooked Melissa's favorite dinner: roasted chicken and root vegetables, in our blue Dutch oven, a favorite gift from our wedding registry. We spent time snuggling on the couch, setting the mood the best we could, but there's only so much you can do to make a syringe feel like rose petals.

Despite the clinical logistics of the "deed," we laid on our backs in bed afterwards with Melissa's legs up on the wall (if you know, you know) and we were giddy. We were officially TTC—trying to conceive.

The negative pregnancy test after an agonizing two-week wait wasn't a huge surprise, but it was devastating nonetheless. And it came with a literal price tag. The vial we'd used, the shipping, the supplies, all tallied up. The receipt was the negative test in our hands, with no guarantees we'd ever see that desperately desired second pink line.

We weren't a straight couple casually "trying." We got one shot a month, if we were lucky. And it wasn't exactly fun.

Even though we still had a number of vials left, a spark of panic was lit: what if it never works for us?

After another at-home attempt, and another negative pregnancy test, we decided to change our approach to Intrauterine Insemination. We had planned for this possibility, so we'd intentionally purchased more IUI vials than ICI vials because the odds of success are higher. Still, we had felt that naïve optimism. We'd hoped we might be one of the "lucky ones" who could conceive at home, with just the two of us and a frozen vial of sperm.

We had already established care with a fertility clinic near us, so taking the next step to IUI at the clinic was easy. Seeing another negative test, though? That part never got easier. As the number of vials dwindled and the months ticked by, the spark of fear that we'd never be parents was gaining oxygen.

By March, we had been on this journey for nine months. We hadn't tried every month—some we skipped to avoid due dates overlapping with important weddings, or for holidays, or to give Melissa's body a break—but we were down half of our precious vials. Regardless, we felt more confident going into our next attempt thanks to everything we'd learned along the way. At least we knew what to expect.

Then Melissa ovulated a few days early.

On a Sunday. When the clinic was closed.

We called the weekend emergency hotline in a panic, and they told us to go in first thing Monday for our IUI. Happy birthday to Melissa.

There was another problem though: Our vial of sperm wasn't scheduled to arrive until the day of the procedure. That said, the deliveries always happened first thing in the morning, so while we were cutting it close, it looked like we'd just pull it off. We went to bed that night, hopeful and ready. Maybe vial number five would be the lucky one.

We adjusted our work schedules so we could take the morning off, woke up with the sun, and hopped into the car for the all-too-familiar drive to the clinic. As the sky brightened, we talked through our nerves. If this one didn't work, we might have to change our approach again.

Then, Melissa received a shipping notification.

"WHAT?! THE SHIPMENT CAN'T BE DELIVERED?!?" she cried out.

My heart dropped, and I had to force my hands to stay steady on the wheel.

"What the fuck do we do now?" I asked, my mind racing. How could this happen? Did we have to ship the vial back? Would we have to wait yet another month? Would I have enough time off at work to keep trying like this? Melissa called the clinic, even though we were almost there. They told us to come in anyway and that we would figure it out.

We continued our drive in silence, losing hope with every mile.

When we arrived, the clinic assured us they were open since 4 that morning, despite the notification we had received saying that our package "could not be delivered, business not open." They advised us to call the shipping company and see if the truck could return later. It wasn't like we could do the procedure tomorrow. The timing of conception attempts is wantonly unforgiving. So, we called. We got no guarantees but just enough reassurance to stay.

The hours ticked by.

We both ended up having to unexpectedly take the day off of work, and the emotions began to set in. This was more than another negative test. This one felt personal. Why was this so difficult? Every attempt required time taken from work, money down the drain, hopes dashed. This felt like salt in the wound. Again, happy birthday Melissa.

Then, we met a nurse who ended up being the closest thing to divine intervention I've ever experienced. We were crying in the lobby, and she asked us to fill her in about what was going on. Without batting an eye, she said "follow me."

We followed her through a labyrinth of hallways. To this day, I don't know who she is, but she was clearly a veteran of the clinic based on the length and vibrance of the gorgeous variety of pothos plants in her office. After we filled her in on the details of our situation, she said, "I know the shift manager at the shipping company. Show me your tracking information."

A few minutes later, she knew exactly what was going on. Not only that but the vial was on its way to us. She explained, "Turns out the usual delivery guy is out sick today.

The replacement driver hasn't made a single delivery all day! Go ahead and take a seat. The manager is heading to the truck now and sending it straight to us."

We couldn't believe it, but we were still cutting it extremely close. The vial had to be delivered in the next hour, or it would be too close to the clinic's closing time for Melissa to have the procedure. As we sat anxiously in the waiting room, watching the clinic empty and staff leave for the day, our hearts gained weight in our chests. We watched the final patient of the day walk in, followed by a delivery driver with our package on a dolly.

If I told you the fertility clinic staff tore this delivery guy a new asshole, that would be an understatement. They shredded this man as if the tank in his possession carried a vital organ for transplant, not a vial of sperm. As a non-confrontational person, I'll admit I was a bit uncomfortable, but it felt good knowing we had people rooting for us. He couldn't care less about the verbal assault. It was clear he didn't care much about his job anyway.

As soon as he left, they showed us to our room. The vial still needed to thaw, but it was here, and the month wasn't wasted.

After confirming all the important details, including Melissa's name and the donor number on the vial, Melissa had her IUI procedure.

Two weeks later, we couldn't believe it when the test finally said "pregnant."

CHAPTER THREE

THE FIRST SIBLING

"It seems like there could be a lot of other kids. Do you think all sperm donors meet these family limits?"

This was a question Melissa and I asked ourselves but never really looked into. Family limits were something we read about on the cryobank websites, but it all felt abstract. How many people are allowed to have children from the same sperm donor? How do they arrive at that number? How many vials are available per donor? They don't make it easy to find out the truth.

By opting to build our family with donor sperm from a big cryobank, we knew in theory that our child would have biological half-siblings, and we hoped we'd be able to connect with them. We imagined it might be helpful for our child to have others in their exact, or very similar, situation to talk to. To just get it. Before our child was born, we were already searching for the people who would understand their story—not because we told it to them, but because they were living it too.

I know what it's like to carry something deeply true about yourself and not have anyone around who fully understands. That kind of isolation leaves a mark. We didn't want that for our child. We wanted to surround ourselves not only with adults who made similar choices to us but also with other kids who were living inside those choices.

Once we were confident in Melissa's pregnancy, I started to scour the internet for ways to connect with the other families that chose Donor 2XC89. I was obsessed with imagining my future kid—so much so that we ordered an early blood test so we already knew he was a boy. I still wondered: would I see my wife in him? What will his interests be? Most families have lots of pieces to help construct an image of their future child, like shared physical features or personality quirks passed from generation to generation. For example, in my family we joke about the "Ramos nap gene" that allows us to nap easily. Things like that! But he wouldn't inherit the gift of mid-day slumber, or anything else (at least not genetically), from me. We were missing about half of that foundational information about our son, but the other children and their families, if we could find them, felt like a way to connect with that side of him.

It felt strange to want something so badly yet have no idea what I was walking into. Would I find pictures of the other kids? Would they look like the donor? Would there be other families like ours? How many were there? What would it feel like to connect?

Time went on. Weeks passed. Then, one afternoon, I finally found my way in.

I should acknowledge that Melissa is deeply involved, but I'm the extrovert in our pair. I've always taken the lead on communicating in this arena, but none of this is ever a solo decision. Every step we've taken has come from long, thoughtful, sometimes teary, often joyful conversations. We keep checking in and making sure we're aligned, making sure we're ready.

"I found a post about our donor!" I told her.

I showed her immediately:

"A few of us made a Facebook group for 2XC89 families. We'd love to connect with any others!"

A few of us? Who were they?!

I don't remember what I was doing when the approval came through—just that suddenly, there it was. The Facebook group for Donor 2XC89.

We were immediately overwhelmed, flooded with stories, photographs and videos of beautiful families and adorable children. We saw babies babbling, toddlers with perfect curls and smiling faces, and parents beaming beside them. I had imagined what it might feel like to see the children, but the reality of it was more emotional than I had pictured. We were expecting a little boy, and here on our screens were a bunch of adorable little faces; faces that might carry the same features as him.

The donor ("Cutie Man", as we called him at this point) still felt abstract, like a checkbox on an order form. But these kids? These families? They were tangible.

And then, a surprising wave of relief washed over me. All of the families were non-traditional. They were all single moms by choice, two-mom households, or queer families like ours. These donor-conceived kids were already living the kind of life ours would grow into. We weren't just included in the group; we were reflected in it. That was something I hadn't realized I was so nervous about. In most spaces, I am the outlier. Here, I was pre-approved. I was galvanized and relieved by the community I saw in front of me.

But there were already 10 children, and 3 more, including ours, were on the way.

Whoa.

Those family limit numbers we'd read about didn't feel theoretical anymore. We realized that we would be watching the number of Donor 2XC89 children and families grow in real time. We were starting to comprehend just how overwhelming it could actually feel when twelve other families were shocking enough. Would there be even more?

We kept reading. Families were spread across the country—West Coast, the South, and the Midwest. I remember trying to picture the map in my head, wondering how many of these kids would ever meet.

Ping

There was a message in my inbox.

It was one of the moms from the group! She introduced herself warmly and told me she had a wife and a nine-month-old little boy, Otto, and that they lived in New York City.

New York City. That's where we live.

I cursed aloud. "HOLY SHIT?!" Then, I messaged back immediately.

There was another family nearby?! What were the odds? I mean, I guess they're better in a place like this—we're in a major city, in a liberal state, with a big population of queer families. But still, it felt like magic. It felt as if the stars were aligning.

They messaged: "Congratulations! We're so happy to have you here! Would you be interested in a hand-me-down bassinet and some clothes for your little one?"

It was happening so quickly. We were going to meet one of the other families?! One of our kid's siblings?! Before he was even born?!

"We would LOVE that. Thank you!" I wrote back, and we got to planning.

A few weeks later, we were in the car and heading to their place. It was surreal. We were still in the phase where all we could do was imagine what our life as parents might be like, and it felt like we were about to get a glimpse into our future. That day, driving across the city to borrow a bassinet from strangers who somehow already felt like family, it began to sink in that this wasn't going to be just our story anymore. Our family wasn't just us and our kid as we'd always imagined it. It was already bigger than us.

We still had no clue what it would look like in the future, much less all the emotions and complexities we'd face as we continued navigating this new terrain, but we were happy to be connected, and others seemed happy to be connected too. We couldn't wait to find out more.

At the time, we weren't thinking about ethics or identity or the stickier questions that would eventually arise. We didn't yet know what we didn't know. We hadn't read the stories or listened to donor-conceived voices. We didn't even know the term "donor-conceived person" or the acronym DCP. We just knew we wanted a support system for our son, and somehow, it was already coming together.

We pulled up in front of a fire hydrant (because, New York), popped on our hazards, and texted: "We're here."

And then, so were they. A gorgeous family. A beautiful, bright baby boy. Hugs all around.

I can't remember what we talked about, but I remember how it felt. Easy. Outstanding. I remember their excitement for us and the fact that we lived so close. I knew a few other queer families with children, but this was something different. Not only would my son know some of his siblings, but he'd be growing up alongside one. We were so excited to know them. And in a strange way, we already felt like we knew *him* a little better by extension.

Something about it all hit me harder than I expected. The photos of the kids in the group, the messages from other parents—they reminded me of how lonely it felt growing up without mirrors. I spent so much of my life explaining who I was or avoiding being seen altogether. What I really wanted, what I still want, is to just show up and be understood. And that's what happened here, among strangers bound by a monumental (and seemingly random) set of circumstances. I felt more immediately seen than I'd ever been.

That, I realized, was what we were trying to give Riley by connecting with this group: a shortcut to belonging. A chance to feel seen from the start. We had no clue what our future with these new connections might look like, or what a profound impact this new community would have on our family, but we knew we were scratching the surface of something much deeper. I didn't yet know how deep this journey would go—how much I'd come to learn from donor-conceived people (DCP) or how my understanding of ethical family-building and the fertility industry at large would evolve. But I was reaching out with earnest curiosity, tilling soil and planting seeds of an unknown variety.

We had four months left of Melissa's pregnancy. Our baby wasn't even born yet.

But already, he had people. And so did we.

CHAPTER FOUR

WELCOME, RILEY

One of the first things I grappled with as a newly-out nonbinary person was language. The words I used were all in flux—how I described myself, the name I used, my pronouns. In 2015, nonbinary identities weren't widely recognized. The word "nonbinary" wasn't even part of the cultural vocabulary yet, so I had very few examples to show me the way.

The term that first cracked something open for me was "genderqueer," and that's how I identified in those early years. It was amazing how hearing the word was all it took for everything to change. The instant I heard it, I knew that was me. It became one of many examples in my life where language has been integral to identity. But, while I was gaining comfort with my identity as a nonbinary person, I didn't yet know what it would mean for my future romantic relationships.

In 2016, I wrote in my blog:

"Am I allowed to exist in lesbian circles as a nonbinary person? How do I find potential love interests? When I do meet someone to date, what would even they call me? I don't like the word partner. Can I just be their person?"

Without knowing it, when Melissa finally asked me to be exclusive, she said exactly that: "Be my person?"

I had waited patiently for that moment. While I was ready to commit to a relationship with Melissa pretty quickly after we began dating, she needed some time to be sure. Although I was bummed, I wasn't upset that she didn't want to label it. I was just glad that she wanted to continue spending time with me at all.

On our second real date, my newfound confidence caught me by surprise. We were at a bar having drinks and playing "truth or dare" Jenga. It wasn't an actual, formal game. Just boxes of Jenga blocks that had been scribbled on through the years by patrons like us. There were random "truth" questions and/or dares written on each block. It made for such a great early date spot because it pushed us out of our comfort zones.

Halfway through the game I pulled a block with a single, simple dare spelled out on it: *French Kiss*. I was…flustered. I felt heat rise to my face and stuttered something along the lines of "uh maybe that one's for later" and pulled out a different block instead. Unbeknownst to Melissa, I slipped the *spicier* block in my pocket with a plan I wasn't sure I could actually pull off.

Later that evening, once again far too late for a work night, we were saying our goodbyes. I pulled the Jenga block from my pocket and handed it to her, asking, "Can I cash in on this one now?"

I swear to you, I am NOT a smooth person. This is probably the suavest thing I will ever do in my life.

After a few more dates and many more deep conversations came the moment I had been waiting for. Melissa handed the Jenga block back to me, but this time, on the other side of the block, she had written: *"Be my person?"* And thus, my love for her was cemented.

Melissa was the first person I dated after changing my name and pronouns. I had so many questions in my head about what a partner would call me, what my relationship would feel like, how gendered or heteronormative assumptions and experiences might factor in now that I was straddling genders. Luckily, Melissa was exactly who I needed. She asked such thoughtful questions—and always from a place of kindness and genuine curiosity. She helped me find confidence in myself, especially in how I related to others. I was so confident in who I was internally, but having acknowledgement of my identity and validity from a romantic partner was the final piece of the puzzle. It was the piece I needed to truly love myself.

A few years after our fateful Jenga date, as our friends and family set up a surprise engagement party at our favorite neighborhood restaurant, I gave Melissa the Jenga block back again, another new question now written on the side: *"Will You Marry Me?"*

It took me a while to find language that felt like it fit, both for my relationship with Melissa and for myself as an individual. I sat in the discomfort of not having the right words, hoping they'd come eventually, and eventually feel right. But even now, the question keeps resurfacing simply because our society still isn't built to accommodate people like me. As we continued on our parenthood journey I began to wonder: If I had a kid one day, what would they call me if not mom or dad?

Like many baby gays of my era, my earliest model of queer parenthood was Bette and Tina or "Mama B" and "Mama T," as their daughter called them, on the TV show *The L Word*. It's funny to look back on now, but it planted a real question for me: What words work for our family? I would certainly never be a "Mama E."

By the time Melissa and I were thinking seriously about parenthood, we had a few queer families at our family daycare. One stood out to me. They went by "Dada" and "Abba" with their son. I later learned that "Abba" is a version of "dad" in Aramaic and Hebrew, but what struck me was that it didn't feel gendered to me. It was just…a parent word. One I'd never heard.

My sister helped me take the final step. One day she said, "What if you used Abba as inspiration, but made it personal to you? What about Eba?"

And just like that, Eba (ee-buh) was born.

Years later, I learned that the Hebrew word for mom is Imma (pronounced ee-ma), making Eba an accidental phonetic mashup of existing words for mom and dad, just from a different language. It was a nonbinary word—both and neither. It felt like another one of those quiet, kismet moments.

I first practiced being Eba when we rescued our pandemic puppy, Liberace. I was his Eba before I was anyone else's. I didn't realize it then, but it ended up being the perfect way to introduce the idea softly and casually. I got to explain and explore the word with friends and family, and it always just felt like me.

Still, I wonder sometimes, would my life, and my son's, be simpler if I'd picked a word people already understood? Honestly, yes. But such a word doesn't exist in a way that feels natural. I wouldn't want my kid yelling across the playground, "Parent! I need help!" It just sounds ridiculous.

Language, and my own experience as someone who uses a chosen name different from the one I was given at birth, is part of why we chose a gender-neutral name for Riley. Even though we are using the pronouns that align with his assigned sex at birth, we didn't want his name to define him in a chromosomal way. We wanted to leave space for exploration and possibility.

To me, the flexibility of language mirrors the flexibility of self. It offers room to grow and change. I hope that having a gender-neutral name gives Riley permission to discover who he is without feeling boxed in by it, something I didn't have growing up.

Claiming my parent name was an even more profound act than choosing my own name. Eba is both a name and a title. It's not something I inherited; it's something I created. It is a word that holds both who I am, and the role I love most. I hope it helps model for Riley the power of language, and of naming yourself.

So, I knew what my child would call me, but I still had plenty of questions and fears. Melissa was Riley's genetic and gestational parent, so I wouldn't be biologically related to him. What would our relationship be like? How would I feel holding him for the first time? Would we be close? Would we have anything in common? I knew I would be his parent, and that I would love and care for him no matter what, but the questions lingered. I'm sure all parents have them, but there's an extra layer of uncertainty when you don't have the built-in reassurance that shared genetics can provide.

It left me feeling a little disconnected from Melissa during the pregnancy. Being a non-gestational parent is hard, especially as someone living with anxiety. I was immediately filled with worries after the positive test, both about the pregnancy itself and about my relationship with my future child. My anxiety is the kind where (unbeknownst to Melissa) I googled the statistical odds of miscarriage every single day of her pregnancy until the coveted 26-week viability mark. For whatever reason, watching the odds change from 2.9% to 2.8% made me feel better. So much is out of your control during pregnancy, so having statistics (especially in our favor) helped me quell some of my more terrifying worries.

I imagine even genetic non-gestational parents feel some distance from their child in utero while they watch from the outside as their partner builds an intimate bond with the baby growing inside of them. I felt like I would be starting a few steps behind, already trying to catch up in terms of connection. It wasn't that I doubted my ability to parent a child who wasn't genetically mine, or that I didn't gestate. I just worried, deep down, that I might never fully live up to the title of "parent" somehow when Melissa already was, and so beautifully.

Two days past our due date, Melissa began bleeding. I texted my sister, asking if she could come watch our dog in case it was go-time, and we made our way to the hospital. Luckily, when we arrived, they assured us that the bleeding was normal and that all it meant was that Melissa had begun labor. They officially checked us in to begin the birth process.

Time moved sideways, with the mixture of anxiety, medical personnel, and procedures. I was incredulous at every insistence that we try to *rest*. How? I was so focused on Melissa, anticipating erratic contractions to the best of my abilities, and thinking about finally meeting my son that I didn't have time to think about any of the other worries that had plagued me during the pregnancy, much less sleep (Ramos nap gene be damned).

All of a sudden, the fetal heart monitor went quiet. A group of doctors rushed in to whisk us into the operating room. Our worst fear came to life in the blink of an eye: an emergency c-section.

As the surgery began, I held Melissa's hand. Neither of us could believe what was happening or that we were finally about to meet our child. I'd heard so many stories about the overwhelming emotions new parents feel, and I wasn't sure I'd feel them myself, especially given the circumstances. Not every parent does, and that's okay, but to my surprise and relief, I did. Every doubt I'd had vanished the moment the doctor asked, "Are you ready to meet him?" and popped him over the curtain separating us from the surgery happening just feet away. I instantly cried harder than I ever had in my life, enough to even make the OR staff a little concerned. I was overwhelmed by my love for this tiny new person and for Melissa, his incredibly strong mother.

As Melissa had her first skin-to-skin snuggle I texted the various group threads announcing the healthy birth to our anxious friends and family. Then, I held my child for the first time.

I couldn't stop looking at him. I didn't care who he looked like or what color his hair was. None of it mattered except that he was here and healthy. I knew, with full certainty, that I would love him unconditionally, for the rest of my life.

But almost immediately, I was confronted with gendered assumptions. Every new nurse after a shift change called me "mom." I also lost count of the comments about how "involved" I was compared to most of the dads they'd seen. It made me deeply sad to think about how many people go through this without the full support of a partner, how normalized it is to expect so little of men as parents, and how gendered expectations shape that dynamic.

In that moment, and many others before and since, I felt so grateful to be queer. Melissa and I don't argue over who should do what. We both know what needs to happen, and we show up for each other to get it done. The roles we take on are shaped by our strengths and our conscious partnership, not by our genitals.

Parenting, for us, was the same beautiful balance our lives had always been. We've always communicated well by voicing our needs and stepping in for each other without keeping score. We felt solid in our relationship and confident in our roles as parents. But we were constantly reminded that, to the outside world, we weren't a "traditional" family.

"Do either of you have food allergies?" our pediatrician asked after we discovered our son's egg allergy—forgetting, in that moment, that only one of us was genetically related to him.

"We have to do trainings about families like yours every year, but the owner just doesn't get it," our son's (short-lived) daycare teacher told me casually at pick-up one day.

"Your mom."

"Your mama."

"Your mommies."

My son wasn't even a year old, and already the complexities of being donor-conceived, and of being the child of queer parents (including a nonbinary one), were showing up in our daily lives.

It's hard to put words to the pain I felt, knowing that from the very beginning, my son would see the world fail to recognize me for who I am. That I would be something else to them. Something…other.

I was used to managing these situations on my own by reading people to decide whether I cared enough to correct them, or whether they felt safe enough to tell the truth to. But realizing that my son would inherit that same burden, just by being mine, was both humbling and heartbreaking.

I know that Riley's journey is out of my control. He very well may feel ashamed of me, or of us, at some point in his life. He may resent not coming from a more traditional family. I'm trying to prepare myself now not to take it personally if it does happen.

But I also know that I want him to grow up with a sense of honesty. Without shame or confusion about who he is, and how he came to be. I want him to know and feel empowered by his story, not burdened by it. And as much as the world may label him and us as "other," I'm committed to making sure he always knows that he is loved exactly as he is and that the way he came into the world is just one part of a much bigger, more beautiful story.

That's why I'm choosing to be open about the sperm donor Melissa and I chose and about Riley's half-siblings—even when it's not easy or when it brings up my own discomfort or fears about our family. Because I want Riley to grow up knowing the truth. And I want that truth to feel natural, like it's just part of our story and never something to hide.

Riley met his hand-me-down bassinet half-brother Otto when he was just three months old. It was incredible. We gathered in our little apartment in Brooklyn, reveling in the craziness of parenthood and marveling at the circumstances that brought us together. They got to hold Riley, we got to play with Otto, and we spent a few hours together in parental bliss. We'd been in the Facebook group for months at this point, but now we had a child in the group. We were finally, officially, parents, and we had other parents in our corner from the start.

More families slowly trickled into the group, and by the time Riley turned one, we knew of twenty other families—three of them in NYC. One of the newer nearby families was open to a get together with our family and Otto's family, so we planned a playdate for three of the Big Apple kids. Then came another bit of kismet in the form of a text from another group mom: "Hey NYC families! I'll be coming down for a work trip with the kids. Anyone want to meet up?" The date she suggested? The exact day of our already scheduled playdate. We picked a gathering spot in Prospect Park, and got ready to gather with FIVE of the half-siblings.

I went into that day full of excitement and nerves. It would be Riley's first time on the subway too, so the logistics of traveling helped distract me from the deeper anxiety of meeting new people (a little extra anxiety inducing since Melissa wasn't able to join). I'm pretty extroverted, but I also live with anxiety and depression. Walking into new groups has never been easy for me—maybe because I've so rarely walked into one and felt like I truly belonged.

This group was different, though. These were fellow queer parents. So why was I still so nervous? Because this wasn't just a playdate. These were my son's siblings. He was meeting three of them, and their families, for the first time. These relationships could shape his life. They might shape mine. Still, it wasn't until I set foot in Prospect Park that my heart really started to race.

It was, like the first time, incredibly easy. Everyone was warm, welcoming, and genuinely excited to be together. Riley was still asleep in the stroller when we arrived, which even gave me a chance to properly meet everyone before the chaos kicked in (something I definitely took for granted before having a kid).

When he woke up, I plopped him onto the grass next to one of his half-siblings. What happened next caught me completely off guard. They leaned into one another, forehead to forehead, smiling at each other like they shared a secret language only known to babies. It was simple but profound. They were immediately comfortable together. And so were we, the parents.

The afternoon flew by. Our kids shared snacks and belly laughs while we chased them around the park, constantly in awe of the strange and beautiful chain of events that brought us to this moment. Having such an intimate commonality, Donor 2XC89, gave the moment a certain gravity. We were watching the beginnings of something rare, real, and completely unexpected. None of us parents knew what these relationships would mean. None of us knew what the future would look like. None of us had examples to lead the way. But we were here, we were in this together, and we were creating a new way forward.

Even when we weren't together, we kept the momentum from that first meeting. Families were sharing more in the Facebook group and starting to have deeper conversations. We continued meeting up with the NYC families and asking questions to define these new relationships and learn how to do best by our kids.

And then, one of Otto's parents opened a door to a whole side of donor conception that I was ill-informed about: "I highly recommend you check out the Facebook Group *Donor Conceived Best Practices and Connections.*"

Joining that group was such a big turning point that I think of my understanding of donor conception as before versus after the group.

That's when I stopped thinking like a parent who used a donor and started thinking like the parent of a donor-conceived child.

CHAPTER FIVE

LEARNING FROM DONOR-CONCEIVED PEOPLE

"Donor Conceived Best Practices and Connections is a group for Donor Conceived People, Intended Parents, Recipient Parents, and Donors of eggs, sperm, or embryos to come together to work towards the betterment of the lives of donor conceived people in our families and communities."

When you first join the group, you're asked to self-mute for fourteen days and just listen. I'm so glad that rule exists because the topics are heavy, and the opinions are strong.

"Children deserve access to their biological families."

"Our sibling group is in the hundreds."

"The cryobank lied to us about our donor's health."

"All donor conception is unethical."

My initial reactions to the group were very different to how I feel now. I imagine many recipient parents who find themselves in the group ride the same emotional wave I did in the beginning: shock, fear, insecurity, horror, bewilderment. There was just so much to take in—hundreds of posts, links to books and documentaries, language guides, threads about legislation, etc. All of it opened my eyes to a side of my son's life I had barely begun to understand, and forced me to confront my own insecurities as a queer, non-biological, and recipient parent.

As overwhelmed as I was, I knew right away that I had to learn as much as I could. I had no clue that some of these opinions existed, much less where they were rooted. I realized that in order to support my son, I first needed to work through my own discomfort. If I wanted to be the best parent I could be, I had to dive headfirst into the hard stuff. So, I kept reading. And I started looking for more. I found (and rapidly began consuming) podcasts, documentaries, tv series, and books. Once I realized how much I didn't know, I couldn't stop. Honestly, I still haven't.

I remember the first big sting I felt from something I read in the group. It came while I was reviewing the list of banned and preferred terms: "social parent."

Oof.

There it was, listed as one of the banned terms, but it hit me right in my most tender spot—the one that secretly worried that I'm not a *full* parent because I don't share DNA with my child.

I hadn't expected it to hurt as much as it did. I am confident in my relationship with my son. I know I'm his parent in so many of the most meaningful and important ways. We have an absolutely incredible bond. But something about that word —*social*— made me feel immediately lesser, like I needed an asterisk next to my title. It made me feel like I was "just" the parent who showed up, not the one who belonged. Once again, an "other."

Even if it was a word people weren't supposed to use, a word no one directed at me specifically, it was cutting.

I also learned that some of the language I had been using was not preferred by donor-conceived adults. Words like "dibling" (short for donor sibling) that I once thought were cute and unique, could actually be painfully dismissive to donor-conceived people. Some DCP feel that using a word like "dibling" in place of existing words like sibling or half-sibling can both infantilize and detract from the potential importance and reality of these relationships. Their siblinghood is biological fact, as it is with everyone who shares a genetic parent, regardless of how it came to be.

The language was the first part I really explored, because I know firsthand how integral language is to identity and respect. I started to shift:

"Diblings" became siblings, half-siblings or donor-conceived siblings.

"Our son's donor" became: Our son's biological father or our donor (never our son's).

I even started to question industry-standard language like "donor." Can someone truly be called a donor if they are paid for their…services?

At first, it felt like I was being corrected for something I didn't even know was wrong, which is always a humbling and uncomfortable experience. But the more I listened, the more I was reminded that language isn't just about semantics; it's about dignity. If I wanted to honor the lived experiences of donor-conceived people, I needed to not only listen to them, but accept that what they were telling me mattered. This wasn't about being "right." It was about showing up with humility, curiosity, and care. Words like "dibling" or any of the "silly" or "cute" ways I've heard parents refer to their donors, like "seed man," can detract or distract from the factual, genetic relationships between people. We were using real words with Riley for body parts like "penis" to remove mysticism and shame around bodies, so I had to ask: Why is it uncomfortable to use real words here as well?

One of the things that became clear early on was that any level of mystery around one or both biological parents can be experienced as a trauma by the donor-conceived person. For decades, the prevailing advice from doctors and fertility professionals was to keep donor conception a secret from the children produced as a result. "No one needs to know," they said, as if their "professional" advice could outweigh factual biological implications. Reading the voices of donor-conceived adults made it painfully obvious that this historical, intentional secrecy doesn't protect children; it protects their parents. And while that secrecy can protect parental egos, the idea/image of a nuclear family, and fertility professionals, they can also fracture a donor-conceived person's sense of identity, belonging, and trust.

It would be so much easier for me if that weren't true, if Donor 2XC89/Riley's biological father could be someone who mattered only at the moment of conception, and not beyond. If love alone could define family. You'll remember, we went into this journey choosing the cryobank because it felt like the easiest way to have a family that belonged just to us. But the deeper I got into my learning, the more the phrase "love makes a family" started to feel like "I don't see color" in conversations about race. You can't acknowledge that something is real—that every person has two biological parents or that race and skin color shape our lives—and then try to erase it with something more comfortable. It doesn't work that way if you're trying to do right by the people most impacted.

Some argue that biological connections aren't always central to a child's well-being, pointing to more typical conception situations where a parent later passes away or leaves. I completely understand the instinct to compare in an effort to make sense of this unfamiliar terrain, but there are major and inescapable differences. The main difference is that most donor-conceived people are born without the option to know at least half of their biological relatives, intentionally, from the start. Their origin stories are shaped long before they're born by decisions made in cryobank boardrooms, fertility clinics, and private living rooms, and these decisions are often made without a full grasp of what those choices might mean for the future child (and eventual adult). They're treated more as a product than as a person.

What I've come to understand is that while love and intention matter immensely, they cannot erase a person's right to know where they come from. That right doesn't disappear just because a system was built to (attempt to) make it so or because it would be so much more convenient for recipient parents if it wasn't true.

To add to the complexity, the very technology that now makes anonymity impossible to guarantee for donors also makes it easy for our children to search (and potentially find) their biological parents long before they turn eighteen. I signed a contract with our cryobank saying we wouldn't contact Donor 2XC89 outside of their established channels. But my son didn't sign that contract. What obligation does he have to suppress whatever natural curiosity might arise between now and his 18th birthday? What right do any of us have to ask that of him?

The explosion of at-home DNA testing companies like 23andMe, Ancestry, and others has made it abundantly clear that the desire to understand our genetic origins is not a fringe interest. For many of us, it's innate or instinctive. It's not a rejection of love or a failure of nurturing. It's simply part of what it means to be human—seeking connection, understanding, and truth about who we are and where we come from. I myself was gifted an Ancestry kit and took it with extreme excitement to learn more about my particular genetic makeup, and I already know all my genetic relatives.

The difficult thing for many donor-conceived people is that they are impacted, deeply, before they even have a voice. By dismissing the potential significance of biological heritage, well-meaning parents, simply following the advice they were given (or trying to protect themselves from uncomfortable truths), could end up cutting off their children's identity development at the knees.

I started hearing stories from people who hadn't known they were donor-conceived until later in life, and their words brought this reality to life in a profound and heartbreaking way. I heard from one guest on a podcast called *Insemination*, hosted by donor-conceived activist Laura High, who had been convinced she was switched at birth before she knew the truth of her donor conception:

> "There [are] so many donor-conceived people who swear—they're like—I knew something was up. I was switched, I was adopted…maybe my parent had an affair, like they know something is up…I used to, at night after my parents went to sleep, sit there and look at photos. I would, like, take them out…and look at photos of me like fresh out the womb versus like three days into the hospital and say like when did it happen?…it was between the ages of 12 and 18. I was doing this regularly. I was literally a child. And on top of that, for whatever reason, like, I felt like I had to keep this a secret from my parents."[ii]

It became clear to me that donor-conceived people can sense that something is off long before they know why. If no one tells them the whole truth, they're left to make sense of that friction alone—and sometimes, with the added burden of feeling the need to protect their parents' feelings. That possibility broke my heart. The idea that my son might feel isolated in his confusion, or feel he had to hide parts of himself to shield me, was unbearable.

So, I doubled down. I renewed my commitment to learn everything I could and to face my own discomfort and insecurities head-on. Because when Riley comes to me with questions, thoughts, or complicated emotions about his conception or his biological father, I want to be ready—not to fix or soften the truth, but to sit with him in it. I don't want to lead with my own emotions. I want to lead with honesty, transparency, and love. But I still have a lot to learn to get to where I'd like to be.

There were more strong opinions in the group to digest:

"Recipient parents should make every effort to establish early contact with their donors/their children's biological parents. Releasing donor identities at 18 isn't enough."

"Donating embryos is akin to creating adoptees."

"Parents should work to create opportunities for half sibling relationships, especially in cases where the donor is not open to contact."

I wondered what weight the contract with the cryobank really held as I read story after story of parents who had reached out to their donors. Some donors were open to contact, even willing to answer questions, provide more insight, or meet their biological offspring long before they turned eighteen. Some of the sibling Facebook groups like ours, apparently, even had the donors *IN* them!

Other formerly anonymous donors were horrified at the suggestion of early contact, feeling violated simply by being found. I wondered if I should look up Donor 2XC89. I longed to call him by a name instead of a string of letters and numbers. In the end, Melissa and I were too afraid to go that far for a variety of reasons. While sibling connections were accepted (even facilitated) by some cryobanks, connecting with donors was explicitly off-limits. For us, the fear of retaliation from the bank was too real, especially with vials still in storage and our hopes of a future child tied to them. So, for now, Riley's biological father would remain a mystery. But at what cost?

We were already well on our way with the last point, connecting with donor-conceived siblings, but I didn't realize some of the reasons why these relationships could be profound and important to Riley. I knew connecting with people in similar life circumstances might be helpful for him down the line, but there was so much more I hadn't considered. Genetic mirroring, for example. This is something I took for granted as someone that knew their biological relatives. I saw myself in both of my parents in different ways: in shared mannerisms, in physicalities, in how we see the world, and that knowing brought a comfort I had never before examined.

On the flipside, there's genetic bewilderment. When you don't have access to the full picture of your biological origins, it can create a sense of searching without knowing what you're looking for (this even happens for people that don't know they are donor-conceived). There can be both wonder and disorientation. It's like trying to assemble a puzzle without knowing what the finished image is supposed to look like.

I was first introduced to the concept of a "Ghost Kingdom" in Angela Tucker's book *You Should Be Grateful: Stories of Race, Identity, and Transracial Adoption.*[iii] She writes of her own experience as a transracial adoptee and professional working with adoptees and their families. A Ghost Kingdom is an internal space where a person (in this case adoptees, but I believe it also applies to DCP) can contemplate the possibility of who their genetic parent/s might be, as well as the "what ifs" and unanswered questions around their conception, life, and identity. Some of our own questions in this vein could be answered by searching for Donor 2XC89. Although we decided not to, we were glad to at least be building connections with Riley's siblings. That way, they could wonder together and reflect on their commonalities.

I understand so much more clearly now that connecting with half-siblings is about recognition and belonging as much as it is about community. Seeing a smile that looks like yours or a shared quirk, a favorite food or talent, could be deeply impactful. Even something as simple as realizing someone else squints the same way when they laugh. I initially thought of these possible similarities between our kids as cute fun facts, almost like a playful little Punnett square genetics experiment. But these small connections can be huge for identity formation, especially for donor-conceived people who are missing at least half of their biological origin story.

I hadn't fully grasped that before. I had always thought about the sibling pod as a community akin to a chosen family, and while that remains true, I now understand it's also a vital source of genetic self-understanding. It's about shared experience *and* shared biology. For some people, that can be life-changing and incredibly affirming.

But here's the thing about biology and genetic mirrors: they come from many individuals. Each of us has a rich genetic history made up of an array of people who contribute to who we are. Our son's biological father, our sperm donor, isn't the only missing puzzle piece in Riley's story. There are biological grandparents, aunts, uncles, cousins—many people who might've held meaning or offered insight into who he is, had the circumstances been different.

That's an uncomfortable thing to reckon with as a recipient parent. There is a whole family, a group of strangers, that could one day mean (and might otherwise have meant) something to my son. But every time I start to feel that discomfort, I ask myself: How must this feel for donor-conceived people? That question always brings me back. It reminds me why it's so important to keep listening.

I realized there was another major reason why making space for another parent in Riley's story felt so uncomfortable to me: because he is male. I already felt a lot of fear about parenting a boy as two non-men, and the idea of introducing a male parent, especially sooner than we'd imagined, hit a nerve. I knew that Riley's biological father might be able to offer him something that I couldn't. Donor 2XC89 and Riley, without ever meeting, share something that I don't. That was hard to acknowledge, and even harder to make space for. I had to confront the gap between what I could offer and what Riley might one day need—without glossing over it, which is my usual instinct (a hard habit to break as someone who grew up steeped in toxic positivity). As I worked to set aside my own emotions, even in the abstract space of this hypothetical scenario, I started to see the possibilities our donor's presence could open up for Riley. These possibilities might serve him more than my need to protect my ego or hold onto the comfort of a semi-"nuclear" family structure.

What kept me grounded, even throughout the emotional mindfuck, was listening—hearing from donor-conceived people who had lived it; learning about the myth-making that can emerge in the absence of information; about how harmful it can be for people to navigate identity without a grounded truth or a safe space to voice complicated emotions. I also learned something I hadn't fully internalized: a deep desire to be a parent doesn't automatically make someone a good one. Parenthood isn't earned through longing alone. It's practiced and refined, over and over again. That's what ultimately reminded me that my role didn't need to be diminished by biology. In fact, it makes my presence, and my commitment to honesty and truth telling, all the more vital.

As difficult as it was to begin working through my emotions, at least that process was within my control. What felt much harder to face were the issues donor-conceived people confront that stem from the fertility industry itself. It's a billion-dollar industry that, to my shock and horror, is entirely self-regulated (at least here in the US).

"I feel like a product that was manufactured to be a certain way."

"I feel like I have to live up to my price tag."

"I wish I could know my siblings more, but there are too many of them."

"I hate that I'll never even know how many siblings I have or who they are. Anyone walking down the street could be related to me."

My own dad recalled a single parent at our family's daycare dealing with behavioral issues in her donor-conceived son. Momentarily in her frustration she blamed the *exclusive* clinic she had chosen for her fertility assistance, shouting: "This is not what I paid for!"

These issues grow even more complicated when sex selection is involved in conception. While it is illegal in many parts of the world to know the sex of embryos before implantation, in the US it remains a legal practice for parents undergoing IVF. Embryos can be genetically tested not only for health but also for chromosomal sex, allowing parents to choose which to implant. I personally believe there are some cases where sex selection can be beneficial, particularly when it helps avoid heritable conditions linked to chromosomal sex. On the other hand, when it's used to express preferences about a child's identity, shaped more by parental desire than by medical necessity, the implications become far more staggering. The knowledge then shifts from a tool of prevention to a mechanism of control, and I believe that shift deserves deep scrutiny, especially as an individual that does not identify with their chromosomal sex.

Elon Musk famously selected a male embryo when conceiving the child who would later become his daughter, Vivian. Reflecting on this, Vivian wrote on Threads: "My assigned sex at birth was a commodity that was bought and paid for," and asserted that by living as a transgender woman, she is "going against the product that was sold."[iv]

My heart aches for donor-conceived people in these situations, where the circumstances of their conception are not just medical or logistical but transactional. Their very existence was shaped by a choice, and that choice (and the people responsible) becomes something to push back against in an effort to live authentically. When the donor conception process defines a child's value, rather than simply explaining their origin, it can leave wounds that are hard to name and harder to heal.

The moment that truly, fully, shattered the illusion of safety I thought I had by choosing a cryobank was when I watched *The Man With 1000 Kids* which documents a serial sperm donor who "donated" through both private channels and cryobanks, fathering hundreds of children across the world. The title of the docuseries alludes to the fact that even he doesn't know how many biological children he has contributed to making.

The series raised a few issues I hadn't considered: the existence of serial sperm donors (even in cryobanks) and the emotional and public health risks of large donor-conceived sibling pods. When one person is the genetic parent to hundreds of offspring, the implications ripple across generations.

I continued to hear real-life stories from donor-conceived people that made the lack of transparency and presence of serial sperm donors even more disturbing, such as stories of accidental incest. These are people who didn't know they were donor-conceived, or who didn't know that one of their parents was a donor, meeting, falling in love, getting married, and even having children with half-siblings. Imagine excitedly sending off your ancestry kit to see how Italian you really are, only to find out that your husband is your half-brother. World shattering is not a strong enough statement.

These were extreme cases, yes, but they underscored just how little information is available and just how much the fertility industry contributes to systemic risk, secrecy, and harm in this space. It shouldn't be radical to ask how many biological children a donor has, but even *cryobanks* don't know. There is no reporting requirement, no follow-up from the cryobank after you make your purchase to see if a baby resulted—unless you store vials or embryos with them, in which case they'll definitely make sure to contact you to collect subsequent payments.

It's all too easy to forget that cryobanks are businesses. They have a bottom line and a clear incentive to maximize profits. On the opposite end of the spectrum, when you're someone seeking donor gametes to build your family, you're vulnerable, emotionally invested, under pressure (imagined or real), and navigating something deeply personal with unprecedented high stakes. That imbalance creates the perfect conditions for people to be misled or to overlook red flags in the hope of building the family they've dreamed of. The cryobanks "help" by burying the red flags along the way.

Here's an example: Family limits don't actually exist. In the United States, there is no federal legal limit to how many children can be born from a single donor. There's also no central registry tracking donor usage. In other words, there are no real safeguards against serial donors or sibling pods numbering in the hundreds. While donors may sign contracts promising not to donate elsewhere, what good is a contract if no one is enforcing it? It's about as good as trusting spit and a handshake.

I learned more about cryobank policies. While I had initially read and trusted family limits stated on websites, I learned that wasn't the full story. The limits were often based on *reported* families (and sometimes they don't include international families). Whether I had overlooked the details of our own cryobank or they had been buried in the fine print, I don't know. But that brought the possible number of families in our group, globally, to a terrifying new level. When these systems rely entirely on families voluntarily reporting successful births, why would cryobanks follow up with the families that buy donor gametes from them to see if it worked? They have no incentive. By the time whatever number of families report births back to the cryobank, there could be dozens more children, unreported, that were born to dozens more families.

These family and birth numbers get further complicated by the technical side of sperm donation. You might assume one "donation" equals one vial. Not true. It depends on the sample's "quality." A single donation, one ejaculation, can be split into a dozen or more sellable vials. Host Laura High sometimes does the math with former sperm donors on her podcast. She will ask them: "How often did you donate? For how many years? How much were you paid per donation?" She then does the math to estimate how much the cryobank made off them. In one example, the donor estimated he contributed around 200 "donations" over the course of five years. Laura's conservative estimate based on industry standards had the cryobank making $900,000 compared to the donor's $20,000 paycheck.[v]

Cryobanks also exploit the natural time lag between families purchasing sperm and families reporting a birth. There's a long window between collecting the first donation and reaching the cryobank's stated family limit. In other countries, there may be a limit on how many families can purchase sperm from one donor. This is one effective method of *actually* keeping family/sibling numbers low.

That's not the case in the USA. A cryobank could have dozens of families buy vials from one donor before the first birth is even reported. Banks do what they can to get donors to come in frequently over a short period of time, banking as many vials as possible as quickly as possible. A cryobank could have proof of twenty-four families out of a "limit" of twenty-five, and sell fifteen more vials to fifteen more hopeful families without going against the (flimsy) promises made—nay, suggested—to families. At every turn I am reminded that volume equals profit—at the expense of everyone else: the donors, the families sold to, and, especially, the donor-conceived people born as a result.

What's even more troubling is what I learned about how cryobanks can be predatory in recruiting donors. They target young people, often college students, who may not fully grasp the long-term emotional and psychological implications of having biological children raised in other families. They dangle easy money and package it with the feel-good idea of "helping others" (they do call it donating, after all), while preying upon whatever matters most to the young person whether that's financing a spring break trip, paying rent or easing the burden of student loans. Popular donors, ones deemed "most attractive" for prospective parents, are especially targeted. Those are the big moneymakers.

These donors are also often too young for certain health

conditions to have surfaced, and that incomplete health picture gets frozen alongside their sperm (or eggs). Every time I go to the doctor for my annual visit, I'm asked, "Any changes on your mom's side? How about your dad's?" For many donor-conceived people, that question is impossible to answer. They simply don't know at least 50% of their genetic family.

I've personally benefited immensely from knowing my parents' health histories. If I didn't know that my mom was prone to Baker's cysts, how my relatives have reacted to different mental health medications, or that Achilles tendon injuries run in my family, my understanding of my own body would be far less complete. Those details, although small and seemingly mundane, have shaped my medical care and self-awareness in real, impactful ways. This lack of information for donor-conceived people has led to major health consequences, in some cases leading to serious illness, disability, and even death.

In 2016, Australia enacted legislation granting all donor-conceived people the right to learn the identities of their biological parents. Known as "Narelle's Law,"[vi] it honors donor-conceived activist Narelle Grech, who died of likely hereditary bowel cancer. After her diagnosis, Narelle became determined to discover her biological father's identity and to alert any half-siblings who might also be affected. Although the law was not passed in her lifetime, Narelle did have the opportunity to meet her biological father—a formerly anonymous sperm donor—six weeks before her death.

Donors themselves may also feel deceived by the cryobanks they work with. One story that's stuck with me is from someone known as "Donor Dylan". He donated sperm when he was very young, only to later discover he was the genetic parent to over 90 children. He's since chosen to open himself up to contact with families who are interested, but he's been open about how misled he feels. He talks about the shock of realizing just how many lives he had a hand in creating. He notes how different it feels to donate sperm while imagining a theoretical 40 kids (the limit he was told by the cryobank) versus actually meeting the human beings, and so many more of them than you had imagined. The consequences are enormous.

He's doing what he can now to show up with integrity, given the circumstances. I'm trying to do the same as a parent.

CHAPTER SIX

THE SECRETIVE HISTORY OF DONOR CONCEPTION

There is a lot of historical context that has helped me understand how we've gotten to this point. Donor conception, initially, was used as a way to "solve" male infertility while preserving male egos, further perpetuating patriarchal family norms. After decades assuming infertility could only possibly be a woman's issue, the first documented donor conception happened in 1884, when a doctor used the sperm from one of his medical students (the one voted to be "most handsome") to inseminate a female patient. She was chloroformed during the procedure and never told what had been done. She believed she'd undergone a fertility treatment that helped her conceive naturally. Her husband, on the other hand, was told the truth by the doctor. He chose to keep the secret.[vii]

In more recent history, the myth of "sperm mixing" was sold to families struggling with male-factor infertility as yet another ego-preserving untruth. Some doctors would mix sperm from the intended father (usually the patient's husband) with that of a sperm donor, claiming that the presence of another man's sperm might somehow "motivate" the intended father's sperm to succeed. Others, spouting similar logic, would recommend copulating at home after an IUI procedure. These were pseudoscientific smokescreens that allowed parents to cling to the idea that their child *might* be theirs biologically. And it gave patients just enough uncertainty to avoid fully confronting the fact that someone else could be their child's genetic parent.

This kind of secrecy and ego-driven decision-making isn't limited to men. Even in cases where couples use donor eggs for IVF, there are examples of "professionals" providing opportunities for people to preserve a sliver of reasonable doubt about their child's genetic origins. In one story I came across, a doctor told his patient that if her eggs didn't look promising when thawed, he could quietly substitute donor eggs without telling her. He framed this as protecting the "emotional considerations" of infertility, as if shielding her from the truth was somehow an act of care. He said it wouldn't matter anymore once the child was in her arms. But what about for the child?

This same secrecy shows up in families, too. Many donor-conceived people describe their parents' hurtful reactions to them uncovering the truth. In some cases, they are asked to keep the truth of their conception a secret from other relatives, sometimes even from the non-biological parent, to preserve the façade of a "normal" nuclear family. One particularly heartbreaking example from a podcast called *Inconceivably Connected* had the mother asking her adult child not to tell her father what she had discovered about her biological origins because, in her words, "It would upset him too much."[viii]

In moments like these, shame is transferred silently but unmistakably. Parents who haven't come to terms with their own fertility journey hand that unfinished work to their children, asking them to shoulder it instead. Imagine the weight of being responsible for protecting the very adults who should be protecting you. It happens often to children in a variety of ways, unfortunately, but in this case, it is happening by design.

From the start, secrecy and power imbalances have defined this industry. Donor conception has long been shaped by race, class, and social norms. The early clientele were straight, white, married couples, and the donors were chosen to match: straight, white, and often married themselves. In other words, they were seen as "morally upstanding." This homogeneity was one of the factors that made it so easy to keep donor conception a secret. And like most secrets, this one was rooted in shame. Male infertility was seen as a threat to manhood, or a failure of virility. If there was no easy way for a child, or eventually adult, to find out the truth, why tell them? The lack of diversity in sperm donation echoes today. The majority of donors are still white, still of a certain body standard, and, get this, straight.

Gay men are not allowed to donate sperm to cryobanks in the United States. This FDA regulation is a relic of the AIDS epidemic. *All* donated sperm is required to go through a quarantine period and mandatory testing, including for HIV. There is no real reason why gay men (or bisexual, or queer, or men who have sex with men) should still be excluded from being sperm donors, yet they are. How despicable, that this industry which has increasingly profited off of the LGBTQ+ community categorically excludes them as worthy of passing on their DNA. They are simultaneously capitalizing on, and perpetuating our "otherness." It was horrifying to realize that not only were we a part of a system that was designed to erase differences, but we had contributed to it.

The shame baked into this framework doesn't exist only in the male sphere. Many families who conceive with the help of donor gametes wrestle with fears about their child's genetic parent(s). In our case, as queer or single, non-male parents, many of us are reckoning with what it means to raise children without fathers in the home. Some hear that and assume our children are missing something integral. Others rush to insist that one loving parent is all a child needs to thrive or point out the existence of other males in their life. "But he has a grandpa. Isn't that so nice?!" While these platitudes are well meaning, they are also attempts to distract from the truth (intentional or not). What I've learned through this experience is how important it is to hold multiple truths at the same time and not rush through the uncomfortable ones.

Riley is growing up without a father in his home. He also has a loving family who care for him deeply. He may one day be curious about his biological father. If and when that curiosity arises, in whatever shape it takes, it will not diminish what we have as a family. There is room for any and all feelings without any one erasing the others. This space is neither defined nor confined. We're challenging and subverting established norms. We are queering it.

And yet, it's daunting to realize this work will be constant and ever-evolving. This is just one of many systems we live within that were not built with families like ours in mind. It can feel unsafe to admit fears about not being enough when there are still debates about whether families like ours should exist at all. Sometimes, I feel stuck between self-preservation and progress.

Then came a realization that brought many of these hard truths into sharper focus: I myself would be rejected as a gamete donor. I have a thyroid condition called Grave's disease. It's not life-threatening, but it is heritable and requires lifelong management. That alone would disqualify me from being an egg donor. But does that mean I shouldn't be a genetic parent? Who gets to decide which bodies, which genes, which people are worthy of reproduction? It feels like cryobanks are playing God.

If you are feeling discomfort reading this, you are starting to get the idea. This discomfort has built the more I have learned, and I don't expect it to go away. I expect these conversations to be a part of my life for the rest of my life, partly because of the role I have played in it and partly because I now feel drawn to action. My discomfort is a driver, and it certainly helps me empathize deeply with donor-conceived people.

What does action in this space look like? I started to get an idea after watching *Our Father*, a Netflix movie that follows the journey of Jacoba Ballard after discovering her donor conception. Not only does she discover the truth of her conception, but she discovers that her biological father, unbeknownst to anyone, was her family's fertility doctor, Dr. Donald Cline. Dr. Cline had secretly inseminated her mother, and a horrifying number of his other patients, with his own sperm resulting in over ninety biological children. The people born as a result of his fraudulence inherited not only the burden of their origins, but serious heritable health conditions as well.

Fertility fraud is a whole other house of horrors, and it's one where legislation can, and should, happen swiftly. Fertility fraud describes insemination of a patient, with the doctor's own sperm, without the patient's consent or knowledge. Some patients believed they would be inseminated with material from a sperm donor (either chosen for them or that they had chosen themselves), and some believed they were being inseminated with their partner's or husband's sperm. Cases where patients are inseminated without knowledge of the procedure *at all* are called fertility assault (yes, the first ever donor conception was fertility assault). Fertility fraud is only illegal in a handful of states.

As a result of technological advances and the accessibility of commercial DNA testing, more than 50 doctors have been accused of fertility fraud in the US. Over-the-counter DNA kits have changed the landscape of donor conception irrevocably. Donors and doctors who believed they would remain anonymous forever, and parents who assumed their children's biological origins would stay secret, found their assumptions shattered once their children mailed off a vial of spit to one of the big DNA kit services. Many of these cases are especially troublesome because these fertility doctors served a small local patient population, creating scenarios where siblings could easily interact, or fall in love, without knowing the truth of their relationship to one another.

Although donor conception has existed for over 130 years, you probably haven't heard many stories from donor-conceived people themselves. That's because, for most of that time, they had no way of uncovering the truth if it had been kept from them.

While many cryobanks have come to realize they can no longer promise infinite anonymity to donors, I now see that even arrangements for identity release at 18 are an option that prioritizes the comfort of adults over the needs of the people being created. The logic that built these systems is industry-first. Cryobanks are for-profit businesses, motivated by a bottom line. Profits over people. Profits at the expense of people. Profits via the creation of people.

And donor-conceived people were telling us in no uncertain terms: Donor conception is not a transaction; it's a lifelong identity event, and it should be treated as such.

Taking in all this information was overwhelming. There was guilt, fear, and mourning, a slow realization that our method of donor conception came with a whole set of responsibilities we hadn't understood at the outset. The *Donor Conceived Best Practices* Facebook group was what opened my eyes to how much I didn't know.

Some people criticize the group, saying it amplifies the loudest or angriest voices—ones that don't represent the majority of donor-conceived people. And maybe that's true, but they are voices nonetheless, and I want to hear them. I want to hear all sides of the story: the good, the bad, and especially the uncomfortable truths.

Some recipient parents are offended by DCP stories that are critical of the industry or standard practices. Some opponents of reform/transparency write these donor-conceived people off as simply "angry" or "not well adjusted." What it seems to me, however, is that they dismiss the more negative DCP emotions and experiences to protect themselves from acknowledging reality. It often seems that they are defining "well adjusted" synonymously with "uninterested in biological relatives," which I don't feel is accurate or fair.

That said, I have criticisms of the group too. While I came in with a genuine willingness to listen, it didn't always feel like a space that welcomed growth. Once you were let in, it felt like you were expected to already understand—no questions, no learning curve. I found myself wishing for more spaces where it was okay to not know everything yet. Where curiosity or questioning weren't mistaken for resistance. Where people earlier in their learning journey could come into the space without fear of being shamed for not having arrived sooner or having arrived already knowing.

Luckily, more and more donor-conceived people are speaking up, and their stories vary widely. Some are full of connection and joy, and those stories are beautiful and important. But I also want to hear the hardest stories. I want to sit empathetically with discomfort. I want to be challenged, to process what I feel, and then take all of that—emotion, information, context—and hold it up to my own values. What matters to me? What does this mean for our family? What is our responsibility moving forward?

One of the things that my learning sparked for me was the desire to create books for my son—one about his biological father/our donor, with the information and photo we had from the cryobank, and a second one about his half-siblings. Luckily, when I pitched the half-sibling book idea to the Donor 2XC89 Facebook group, the majority of the other families were on board. I didn't want to do it without their consent.

Over the course of the next few months, two other parents and I worked with the interested families to create one page per child (or per sibling pair). Each family shared whatever they felt comfortable including. The pages featured up to 10 photos, including individual and family pictures, and a short blurb about the child with details like their birthday, interests, and where and with whom they live. From the very beginning, I wanted Riley to know about his biological father and his biological half-siblings. I wanted those connections to be part of his story from the start and minimize shame around it. And how lucky we were that so many other families wanted the same, each approaching it in a way that felt right for them.

One of the unexpected joys of the finished sibling book is that it's one of the ways Riley gets to see other nontraditional and queer families like his in an accessible and natural way.

The donor book was trickier. We weren't sure what language to use, especially with Riley still so young and unable to offer input. We pulled ideas from the books we loved, like *What Makes a Baby*, from the ways DCP speak about their biological parents, and from the information the cryobank had shared. Then we took a stab at creating something that could evolve with time. When I say "book," I don't mean anything fancy. It's just a .pdf printed and slipped into sheet protectors in a binder. But it's an integral part of Riley's story, and hopefully just the beginning of the open, honest relationship I hope to build with him throughout his life.

Other families have made their own versions of donor

books too. Having other parents to talk to as we figure this out together has been a lifeline. I'm so deeply grateful we have each other.

Similar to my journey with queerness and gender identity, I have ultimately come to a place of peace with ambiguity. I accept not knowing exactly what the future might hold. I understand that truth, even when messy or uncomfortable, offers a stronger foundation for Riley than myth ever could. And I'm not alone in this anymore; I have examples to follow and people on my team to figure things out with.

Many of us parents in our sibling group community have committed to ongoing learning and listening to donor-conceived people. We advocate for smaller family limits, increased transparency, and meaningful accountability. For legislation that protects the rights of DCP. For counseling support for donors and recipient families before, during and after they embark on this life-altering path. For training for counselors and mental health professionals to help people through it all.

New models of gamete donation are beginning to gain traction, including known donation, where a friend or family member acts as the donor. These arrangements are often presented as an alternative to anonymous cryobank systems, with the hope of addressing some of the issues rooted in the for-profit fertility industry. Is it better for DCP to have access to, or even a relationship with, their biological parents from the beginning? Probably. But these arrangements can be complicated. They can bring up fears for intended parents about custody, financial obligations, estates, and the loss of parental control. They demand a different kind of relationship, one where intended parents make space for another meaningful presence in their child's life. It was a choice that I had once and chose not to make.

Would I make the same decision now that I did then? Yes, but only because it brought me my son. It's another strange dichotomy, criticizing an industry that I have gained so much from.

So, what does the future of donor conception look like? Where do we go from here?

These are questions that will only be answered with time, humility, and a conscious effort to do better than those who came before us.

When I printed out the sibling book, I was hit with a strange mix of emotions. Over twenty-five gorgeous pages. But it was… a lot. So many faces. So many families. So many interests and birthdays. It was beautiful and overwhelming.

Melissa and I saw things differently now, as I shared my new knowledge with her. We understood that large sibling pods, which ours was quickly becoming, can present real challenges for the people within them—especially for the donor-conceived children navigating what all of this means. What struck me even more was that our group only represented the families who had chosen to connect. There were surely others out there we didn't know about…and might never know.

It's an uncomfortable truth we'll always carry, but we're not carrying it alone. We're in this together, showing up, asking hard questions, and ultimately, trying to do right by our kids. I know that counts for something.

And soon, we were about to take our sibling connections to the next level. Melissa, Riley, and I had the chance to join the second annual sibling gathering (we weren't able to go the first year). We would be flying to Oregon, where we'd meet nine more of Riley's half-siblings, and their families, for the very first time.

Our tickets were booked, and we carried a brand-new set of nerves to match the new set of people we were about to meet, but we were proud to be showing up. We were proud to be taking intentional action with the new knowledge we had—and building community along the way.

Eli Ramos

CHAPTER SEVEN

OUR FIRST SIBLING GATHERING

The Donor 2XC89 Facebook group was started by the three first families to find each other (I call them the "OG 3"). They had found one another through a platform called the Donor Sibling Registry (DSR), which connects donors, recipient parents and donor-conceived people. After they got acquainted, they decided to create the Facebook group for any other Donor 2XC89 families who may want to connect. Facebook has become one of the major platforms for recipient parents and sibling groups to find one another because there is no cost barrier, unlike the DSR which costs $99 per year or $199 for lifetime access.

The first big Donor 2XC89 gathering, open to everyone that had connected with the group, happened when Riley was nine months old. We were crushed to miss it, especially since it wasn't far from home, but we had a scheduling conflict. A few days after the gathering, I finally posted in the group to ask how it went. I was tired of waiting for someone to fill the rest of us in! Seeing the photos of so many of the families and children together was incredible (talk about FOMO). Melissa and I knew that we'd do whatever it took to make it to the next one.

Despite missing the first gathering, we still felt so connected to many of the other families through our digital presences. People would post birthday updates, major milestones, and exciting family news in our group. Of course, engagement in the group varies widely—some people are part of the group but hardly engage, while others are more active. That's to be expected in a group our size. Regardless, through Facebook we bonded over shared parenting struggles, our kids' food allergies or picky eating habits. We weren't surprised when Riley started teething early because we knew some of his siblings had gone through the same thing, and their parents had great advice for us. We were building intimate relationships with people we'd never met, and there were quite a lot of them. The ethos of the group aided our comfort and excitement to finally meet more members in person.

We decided to alternate gathering locations each year between the East and West Coasts of North America. It had become increasingly difficult to find a common meeting location given our group size and geographic diversity. By this point, we'd watched the family and sibling numbers slowly but steadily creep up, experiencing a slew of varying emotions along with them. Our Facebook group now included around thirty children, with families scattered across three countries. We put the gathering location up to a group poll, and the votes were sending us to Oregon. We booked our tickets the first chance we got, grateful not to miss out again.

As it turned out, none of the families we'd met so far were able to join, which meant we'd be meeting an entirely new group of strangers; eight families, with nine children in total. Some lived locally or had family nearby, so we decided to book an Airbnb with three of the other out-of-town families and hope for the best. We were full of anxious excitement, wondering if it would feel as easy and natural with these new connections as it had with the families we already knew. I had hardly spoken to the families we'd be staying in the house with. Meeting up for a playdate was one thing, but sharing a house for four days was another. Regardless, Riley was at such a delightful age, 20 months, and we couldn't wait to see how he would interact with his half-siblings.

We were the first to arrive at the rental, a welcome surprise after a long flight. You know how they say the camera adds 10 pounds? A toddler adds 10 hours—at least, that's how it feels when you fly across the country with one. We were grateful for a few minutes to unwind but already impatient for the others to arrive so the long weekend could finally begin. We texted our group chat: "We made it! There's plenty of parking spaces. Text when you arrive and we can help you bring stuff in!" They couldn't get there fast enough.

When the first mom arrived, travel-tired toddler in tow, we greeted each other with exuberant hugs as the kids exchanged cautious hellos. The excitement grew alongside our comfort, and the energy only amplified with each new family's arrival. At last, we were together unpacking, snacking, and letting the kids run wild in the backyard, finally living the trip we'd looked forward to for so long.

We didn't waste a moment. That very first night, some of the local families from the group joined us for dinner at the rental, bringing over lots of games and toys for our kids to enjoy. Thank goodness for that because toys were not high on our priority list for packing. The evening unfolded in a beautiful haze. We could finally match real people to the social media profiles we'd come to know so well. Discovering our children's shared features, quirks, and interests online had been fun, but seeing them in person was more magical than I ever imagined.

The kids settled in quickly, both into the house and into each other. The same was true for us parents. There is an ease that I feel in groups of fellow queer people that I don't feel anywhere else, and this group was no exception. Over the next four days, our shared values and unexpected commonalities kept surfacing in small, surprising ways, deepening the sense that we'd found something rare and unique.

One of the first things this trip reminded me of was how much I love being around children. Our family daycare hadn't survived the COVID pandemic, closing its doors in 2021, and in recent years I'd been working with adult students. Being surrounded by little ones again brought a kind of joy I hadn't realized I'd been missing. But this time, it felt different. These weren't children we'd care for and eventually send off to kindergarten. These were my son's siblings. They shared a biological parent but came from different families, different homes, different lives. And yet here they were, running in and out of rooms together, fighting over toys, sharing snacks. These were children we'd get to watch grow up, children who might matter in our son's life (and our lives) for the rest of our lives.

Something else became clear almost immediately: our parenting and lifestyles meshed in a way that felt seamless. Those of us sharing the house settled into a rhythm surprisingly quickly, even with jetlag, different routines and kids of different ages. Whether we were navigating the zoo, corralling strollers at the aquarium, or cooking dinner at the rental, our similarities kept surfacing. We found common ground not just through our kids but as people. The ease between the children mirrored the growing connection between us, and it started to feel less like coincidence and more like something intentional. It felt like if we'd met at a playground or through school or mutual friends, we might have chosen each other anyway. Instead, we were brought together in this strange, serendipitous way, through a complete stranger. And somehow, it felt just right.

We bonded over our coming out stories, over experiences with religion, over the decision to become parents, over how we chose our donor. We talked about Brené Brown and Dr. Becky Kennedy and about the kind of parents we wanted to be. About how we were determined to do things differently than our own parents had, to break the cycles of silence, dishonesty, and conflict avoidance we grew up with. We spoke of how we want to think more critically about the systems we are a part of and actively create better ones for our kids. In so many ways, we were deeply compatible, and where we did differ, we were generous, curious, and willing to hold space for one another.

I was instantly in love with all of the children, too. There's so much diversity in our group—in how the kids look, in their personalities and interests, in the parents themselves, in our family structures and backgrounds. But looking at their children felt, in a strange and profound way, like looking at my own. I knew how much intention had gone into bringing them each into the world. They were deeply, desperately wanted and loved.

We all carried an awareness, whether shaped by our own losses or by stories we'd heard, of how easily things could have gone another way and how uncertain the path to parenthood really is. That shared awareness gave us an unspoken sense of camaraderie. A quiet gratitude. It was dumb luck, perhaps, but still profound that we had these incredible children, and this open, generous group of families to share the journey with.

The trip couldn't have come at a better time for me. I had been diving deep into the fertility industry, learning everything I could about donor conception, and I knew the other families were on similar journeys and eager to understand more as well. Over the weekend we had so many deep conversations about the donor, about the ever-growing sibling numbers, about the strange mix of curiosity and fear. How many other Donor 2XC89 families were out there in the world? How many families and children would there be in the end? One of our biggest fears was: When the donor realizes how many

offspring there are, will he be too overwhelmed to open himself
up to them?

Before I knew better, open ID felt like a promise I could
make to Riley. It felt like Donor 2XC89 knew what he was
getting himself into, so he clearly expects an 18-year-old to come
knocking at his door one day. Now, it feels less certain. Now, I
know that the same shock and discomfort and strange mix of
emotions we are feeling as parents will likely be experienced by
him too. Cryobanks do nothing to prepare donors for the
complexities that arise when their biological children reach out
hoping to learn more. While we watched the group's sibling and
family numbers slowly continue to rise over a period of time,
slightly lessening the shock, he would probably find out about all
of us at once. I can't even imagine how that will feel for him.

It felt like a relief to say these things out loud to others
also living with these concerns. To speak our fears and
vulnerabilities without sugar-coating or second-guessing.
Although none of us really knew what the "right" thing to do
with all this new information about the industry and donor-
conceived sibling groups was, we did know that we were
building something important for our kids and modeling the
hard conversations they may one day have for themselves. We
were showing up with grace and humility, with open ears and
open hearts.

The fear that had accompanied so much of those early
discoveries started to lose its grip that weekend. No matter what
lay ahead, I knew I was glad to be in it with these people. We
didn't just share similar values and hopes for our children; we
shared many of the same fears, too. And somehow, that made
everything feel a little less lonely.

But whatever hard conversations we had were by far
overshadowed by the joy of being together. The love I felt for

their children was reflected right back to mine. Riley got more affection that weekend than he knew what to do with. It amazed me how much trust I felt in these new connections. We parented together easily, taking turns grocery shopping, feeding each other's kids, offering quick relief when someone needed a break or a moment to regroup. I felt seen and supported like never before—not just as a parent but as a person.

This trip, while it will be remembered for many things, will be especially remembered for one pivotal moment. It happened when, casually hanging out at our Airbnb, one of the moms asked the question we'd been skirting around all weekend. The one I'd been too afraid to ask:

"Have you ever thought about looking up the donor?"

And everything changed.

We were staying in the house with one of the "OG 3" moms, Misha, and as soon as the question was asked her face dropped and her expression changed to one of shock and fear. We knew, even before she said anything, that we were about to find answers to so many of the questions we'd been asking privately, whether we were ready for them or not.

Time slowed.

"I actually found out his identity..."

She dropped the first crumb of information to gauge our reactions.

We were ravenous for it. We had all expressed curiosity about the donor but had never talked about looking him up. At least *I* hadn't talked about it with anyone. Melissa and I assumed the others had the same fears we did. But that wasn't the case! Someone had actually searched for, and found, 2XC89. Unlike when we had considered searching for him ourselves, it felt safe to receive the information this way—we weren't the ones who went looking for it. All of us in the house were on the same page: "We want all the information you have."

And boy, did we get it.

It turns out, he was not difficult to find with the information we had from his cryobank profile. Misha knew his name, had updated photos, family photos, even social media handles. There was so much information about him suddenly available, and it was equal parts overwhelming and exciting. We went from the basic cryobank information to more than we could possibly look through in one sitting. It was SUCH a wild mix of emotions. We were so excited to have more context, more photos, more evidence that our donor was, in fact, a real person. And, not only that, but he seemed like the person the cryobank had made him out to be (much to our relief). Still, we also felt strange—even a bit icky. He has NO IDEA that we know all of this about him (and his family), how many of us there are, or how central to all our stories he has become. It felt like both an invasion of his privacy and necessary context to give Riley. If *we* had been this curious about him, I could certainly understand why Riley might be.

But there was more to the story.

Not only did Misha have all this information about him…she and the other two original families had reached out to him.

It was a lot to take in, but here's the gist. Before they created the Facebook group, the three original families jointly made the decision to find and contact Donor 2XC89. They had taken to heart what many DCP have said: Early contact is preferable, and it is not an option cryobanks offer even if donors would be open to it. They decided to take the risk and see if our donor might be willing to become known to the kids in some capacity now instead of when the eldest child turns eighteen.

They reached out via social media, making sure to protect themselves digitally along the way, and received a reply that, basically, he was not open to early contact and wanted to stick to the cryobank timeline. Understandable.

That was when the Facebook group was formed. So, not only was all of this information about his identity known, but it had been known before any of the rest of us were in the group. Before Riley was even conceived.

We didn't talk about it much more as a group that weekend after the initial unveiling. It was so much to take in and we were all processing on our own, or in our couples. Melissa and I were in bed at the end of the day looking at pictures of our donor and his family with such curiosity and relief.

As I had learned about fertility fraud, negligence and assault, I was secretly a little bit worried because Riley does not look like our donor (and there are few siblings he even slightly resembles). Could we have been victims of one of these nefarious practices? When we saw his family, everything made a bit more sense. That moment continued providing us with perspective: if we had harbored those fears, Riley might, too. And if we felt relief seeing these photos, he might, as well.

I was sad to hear Donor 2XC89's reaction, knowing some other donors are open to at least some form of contact— and the positive impact that can have for the offspring—but I was happy to at least know where he stood. I was also happy that, should he want to connect to us in the future, he had a way to reach out. There are unfortunately many examples of cryobanks failing to relay important health updates about donors (or donor-conceived people that share a biological parent) to the people affected. The families asked 2XC89 if he could please let us know if anything changes and said the one thing I would say if given the chance to speak to him: Thank you. That's where the contact ended.

We left the West Coast with so much more than we had bargained for. We had new connections and friendships, new perspectives, and a ton of new information about Donor 2XC89 to wrestle with, including a first name: Michael.

We got on the plane to head home full of sadness that the trip was over. I wished, and still do, that we all lived closer and could get together more than once a year. At least we had families that lived near us and the Facebook group so we could stay connected. Plus, we would have next year, and all the years to come, to look forward to.

This was still only the beginning.

CHAPTER EIGHT

THE BIG SECRET

After landing back in New York and settling back into our routine, the weight of the trip, and everything we now knew about Michael, Donor 2XC89, started to sink in. It still felt strange calling him Michael, like I was saying something I wasn't supposed to say out loud. The information was heavy, not just in content but in context. One of the most complicated feelings was the burden of knowing his identity, and everything else that had taken place after the uncovering, when others in our group did not.

It wasn't abstract discomfort. I'd built friendships with other parents that were not in Oregon with us, mostly through video calls and long message threads since we hadn't met in person yet. We'd spent hours speculating together, wishing we could call our donor by his name and imagining what it might be.

"What if it's something wild, like Zeke?!"

But now, I knew his name…and then some. And I couldn't figure out how to return to those conversations that used to feel fun and light without feeling like I was lying by omission. I wanted to blurt, "Guess what? We can stop calling him 2XC89 now."

At first, I followed the lead of Misha and the original families: not disclosing but not lying either. I can completely understand why they made the decision they did and empathize with how complex the knowledge became as our sibling group got bigger and bigger. Still, that in-between started to feel misaligned with my values. I hadn't been the one to find him or make contact, but I now knew, and that knowledge made me feel responsible in a new way. Since I was not one of the people who uncovered his identity, I felt uniquely positioned to offer the information to others without having to defend how it was found or the decisions made afterwards.

So, I reached out to Misha and asked if she was okay with me sharing what I knew with a few of the families I'd grown close with. After discussing with some of the other original parents, she gave me the green light.

With sweaty palms and a racing heart, I messaged two of the moms I'd grown especially close to through Facebook. I didn't want to spring the news on them or casually drop it into a thread. This felt like a bombshell. So, I wrote each of them to say that I had learned something about Donor 2XC89 during the annual sibling trip and asked if they'd like to talk on the phone or FaceTime to discuss. I wanted to offer the knowledge with consent, so they could decide if and when they were ready to open that door.

They both said yes, quickly and enthusiastically. We talked at length via video calls, discussing everything I knew, the emotions it stirred, the questions it raised, and the ways it shifted the stories we'd been telling ourselves. We talked about what it would mean to finally tell our children his name and show them new photos. How shocking it felt to see photos of his family and have a more complete picture of who he is as a person. About how it felt that not everyone had the information and how to hold it moving forward (a question none of us had the answer to).

After those initial conversations, it was like the floodgates opened. I couldn't shake the feeling that this information was creating an unspoken divide in a group that was never meant to have a hierarchy. Some of us had the opportunity to learn the truth simply because we were in the right place at the right time (although I did learn that at least one other parent had found Michael's identity on her own). That didn't sit right with me. Plus, our kids were at an age where they could easily disclose something accidentally, and that would be an awful way for this to come out.

By then, there were around 30 families connected to the 2XC89 group. Sharing this information wasn't going to be easy or simple, but I knew I was uniquely positioned and willing to be one of the people stepping into the discomfort. I was willing to be the one who said, "If you want to know, I can tell you." And I quickly realized that there would be just as many versions of that conversation as there were families in the group. But at the very least, I believed everyone should know his identity was known by some of us. Whether or not they wanted to learn the specifics could be entirely up to them, but even that felt like a decision too big to make alone.

After expressing my discomfort and desire for honesty, Misha, one of the newly-informed moms, Jocelyn, and I made a plan. We would divide the group amongst us, approach each family, and offer the information if they wanted it.

I painstakingly drafted and edited, then re-edited my outreach message. I finally hit send and sat motionless staring at my screen, trying to prepare for any possible reaction.

"I wanted to reach out and first, say hi and hope y'all are well.

I know this is somewhat out of left field, but in the interest of transparency, a few parents from our pod are

83

reaching out to let folks know that there is some more information available about our donor/2XC89. If you are interested in knowing more about him, I am happy to share any and everything I know, but absolutely understand and respect whatever you'd like.

I at least wanted to reach out and let you know/start a convo!"

It was nerve-wracking, demanding and emotionally exhausting work.

The effort took weeks. Jocelyn, Misha and I continued having conversations with families on our own and coming back to check in with one another, taking deep breaths, and tackling one conversation at a time. In the course of these discussions, a new mom-to-be had joined our group. How should we approach new members with the overwhelming amount of information about our group and Donor 2XC89? We were still figuring it out but included her in our efforts for transparency and offered the information if she wanted it (she did).

The reactions were as diverse as our community. Some people wanted all the information, ecstatic to have it, while some only took tidbits. Others wanted to know nothing at all. Some were thrilled, and some were unhappy he had been searched for and/or contacted. The strange slew of emotions Melissa and I experienced when receiving the information was playing out in different ways for each parent, and each family, but this time with me as the point-person. I got to know folks more intimately, simply because of the delicate nature of this topic. It felt incredibly sensitive and personal and sparked some really important conversations that I've been grateful to have.

It took a long time, but we were finally back on a level playing field. Everyone in our group at least knew that our donor's identity was known and that he had been contacted. We could move forward with more honesty and transparency and start answering the next big question: *What now?*

We needed to find a way to come back together and work through the many questions and emotions uncovered by the new avalanche of information. So, I posted in the group and invited anyone interested in discussing further to join a chat. What followed was one of the most intense conversations I've ever been a part of where we voiced our varying opinions, frustrations and concerns openly over the next few weeks.

Once the space was created, I settled into my unexpected role as facilitator. I agonized once again over word choice, then sent the first message:

> "Hey everyone! Not sure if more folks will want to join, but hopefully everyone has had a chance to see my post and opt-in if they wanted.
>
> I'm not sure where to start because, it goes without saying, there are a million things we could discuss.
>
> I want to say before we get into anything my intention/hope for this space. This is an incredibly emotional, personal, often difficult topic to discuss. I want this space to be one where everyone is free to share without judgement. We will likely have differing opinions and big emotions, and I want us all to be able to hold that space for one another.
>
> I am sure everyone is here with the same goals: connecting with one another as parents/families and discussing how to do best by our kids.
>
> I also want to kick us off by saying: All of the families in our group, including the new mom, have been offered the opportunity to have as much of the available information known about 2XC89 as they like. Not

everyone has chosen to have information.

In this particular chat, everyone knows that the donor's name is Michael and that he was reached out to/is not interested in contact at the moment. Please be cognizant of that in this chat, because I don't want anyone to come into information they don't want.

Thank you all for being a part of this <3"

There were 29 voices in the chat to be heard, well more than half the parents in our group, and we were off. No one held back.

One of the first things we talked about was his family. It was obvious from the information we had (including social media profiles), that he was very close with them. When I first saw that closeness, I considered it to be an amazingly positive thing. That was one of the qualities we had assumed from his cryobank profile, and it was nice to have it confirmed. To boot, we already knew the ways that some of the children resembled Michael, but to see resemblances between our kids and his family members was revelatory. I, myself, look more like some of my parents' siblings than either of my parents—the same, of course, could be true for some of our kids. Seeing it so plainly laid out in front of us was still surprising.

Then another parent brought up something I hadn't considered. We, as parents, tend to see a close-knit family as a trait our kids might inherit—something warm and promising. For donor-conceived people, our kids in this case, seeing that closeness from the outside could stir up a much more complicated emotional response. Here is a family they are biologically connected to yet emotionally distanced from and invisible to. I could immediately empathize with how painful or confusing that might be. And that's exactly why these conversations matter to me; I want to consider everything, whether or not it ends up being part of my or my son's personal experience.

We also wondered: Is Michael so close with his family that he told them he donated sperm? That he has biological children in the world, children who are connected to them as well? From listening to donor-conceived people, I knew that a donor's openness can depend on how much their family knows in advance. I hope that when the first kid reaches out hoping for more information, it won't come out as a long-held secret or a shock. If he has a wife and children of his own, I hope they already know there are genetic relatives out in the world before one of them shows up in an attempt to connect. I've heard stories of people discovering late in life that their parent or spouse was a donor, and the fallout that results can be intense. I hope that doesn't come to fruition in our own experience.

Sadly, cryobanks don't encourage that kind of transparency, and many donors end up compartmentalizing their donation experience and never telling their families which can further complicate things for offspring who seek contact. That emotional complexity is one of many reasons a donor might choose not to open the door to the people they helped to create.

The newly-available photos also raised questions about our donor's Asian heritage. Was his ethnic background exactly what the cryobank described? We wanted to give our kids honest answers about their ancestry, but all we had was secondhand information, not facts. That sparked a conversation we're still having: How do we support our kids in exploring their racial identity? For some families in our group who share those elements of the donor's heritage, it feels more natural. For us, it's something we want to be intentional about but not in a way that feels forced. It's a delicate balance, and we haven't figured it out yet. For now, we keep talking, sharing what we do know about Michael, and leaning on one another. Other parents have recommended beautiful children's books that explore their particular Asian ancestry through food, stories, and traditions. They are peppered in with all our other books, and I'm happy that they are helping us casually introduce Riley to these aspects of his heritage. It's a start.

We had gained our footing in the chat and were having some really important conversations. But now, it was time to dive into the tougher stuff…like whether it was right to contact Michael in the first place. It's hard to say what any of us would've done if we'd been in the same position as the first three families, and with a group our size, consensus was never going to be realistic.

Still, the question needed to be asked: Why and how did the original families decide to reach out to Michael in the first place?

Only those that made it could speak to their decision, and we all knew it was sensitive ground, but they answered honestly and their reasoning didn't surprise me.

They'd reached out to Michael after reading and listening to the voices of adult donor-conceived people. Like me, they'd been on a learning journey that reshaped their understanding of what their kids might need. As a trio of families, they decided that it was in their children's best interest to learn more about Michael and to see if he might be open to early contact. So, they went for it.

Part of what makes this conversation so difficult is that there's no single right answer. Some families believe that they should have honored the agreement we signed with the cryobank. We knew the terms going in, and they argue that the donor profile was enough information to provide our children with. These families believe that reaching out was a breach of

Michael's privacy, and could leave a sour taste in his mouth, jeopardizing our children's chances of forming a connection with him down the line.

Others see it differently. They believe the cryobank contract itself was flawed. They argue that it asked us to deny our children rights in the form of fundamental truths about where they come from and that the system is broken. Even if we didn't understand it at the start, we now feel a responsibility to offer our kids more if we are able: more knowledge, more honesty, and ultimately, more opportunity to understand themselves fully.

This opinion comes straight from adult donor-conceived people as well. One example of DCP advocating for fertility industry reform came in 2019 when, for the first time, a group of donor-conceived and surrogate-born adults shared their experiences at the 30th anniversary of the Convention on the Rights of the Child at the United Nations. They summarized:

> "Most importantly it was seen that practices, both past and present, result in the deprivation of our fundamental rights guaranteed by the Convention on the Rights of the Child—including, but not limited to, rights conferred by Articles 7, 8 and 35. We have the right to identity, the right to family relations, and the right not to be bought or sold in any form. These are rights that signatories to the Convention—literally every country in the world—have a responsibility to protect." (Donor Kinderen, We are Donor Conceived)[ix]

Yet another example comes from a donor-conceived person wrestling with the friction caused when she reached out to her bio dad, a donor, who felt his rights were infringed upon by being contacted. In episode eight of *Inconceivably Connected*, a podcast about donor conception, Erin shares her devastation after her biological father denied her request for contact. The response, which she received from "his employee," included the sentiment which she paraphrased:

> "Technology robs well-meaning donors of their deserved anonymity."

She went on to describe her reaction:

> "Obviously it was, it was...so dehumanizing in a way. It just made me feel...ok so, how he feels matters and how my parents felt mattered...like they signed this contract, but like, I didn't sign this contract and this affects MY health and MY future child's health...And also, it's just not fair. I was crushed."[x]

The fact that *some* donor-conceived people feel their rights have been ignored (nay, denied) by the fertility industry is reason enough for me to believe that change is needed. That better systems can and should be built. That I have a responsibility to reexamine how I first approached donor conception and family-making to create something more centered around Riley's rights and potential needs.

As someone who belongs to multiple marginalized communities, I know what it feels like to be systematically disenfranchised. I have been told that the rights I have, while unequal, should be enough for me. In fact, I, too, have been met with incredulousness when expressing my desire for true equality. So now, I'm trying to understand and listen in earnest to the challenges faced by the community my child belongs to. I consider myself an ally.

That's not to say that people who are approaching this differently aren't also allies—or that they're bad parents, or insensitive to their children's needs. Parenting is deeply personal, and it *should* look different for every child and every family. I'm simply sharing my own journey to show my work and explain the intention behind the choices our family is making. And also, to ask donor-conceived people: Am I getting this right?

If Michael had not yet been contacted, I personally would be in favor of reaching out now. Although I am disappointed that he is not interested in contact at the moment, I'm not surprised. I am at least glad to know where he stands, glad that he knows we exist, and glad he has a way to contact us should he change his mind or should any major health issues arise.

I am also glad that I received this information at the time I did, which was not necessarily the case for all of the other families. I had already been doing a lot of learning from DCP and developing my own opinions and thoughts around what best practices look like for us. I was quickly moving towards greater and greater transparency. Receiving this information after I had already started this learning was a stroke of luck. I'm not sure how I would have reacted had I found all this out when I first joined the group, being already overwhelmed by the number of siblings and families.

For some of the families in our group, learning that the contact had happened two years prior was devastating. Parents like me, hoping to give their children more information about Donor 2XC89, could have known his name/identity this whole time and included it in conversations and in their donor books. Realizing the information was withheld for so long was a difficult thing to talk through, but it was another stone that could not be left unturned.

Again, there isn't a clear right or wrong. The original families did not know any of the rest of us at the point when they made these decisions, and they could not have known how many of us would eventually connect. We approached the conversation carefully, aiming for understanding without scrutinizing:

Why did it take two and a half years for this to come out?

The truth is, they had also been struggling with the weight of the information. Even among the original parents, coming to a consensus about how to move forward wasn't easy. As the group grew, holding the knowledge became more complicated. And, the older the kids got, the more likely it became that one of them might bring up Michael casually in conversation. They knew the information eventually would, and should, come out when the time was right.

Regardless of our opinions on the matter, this exchange with Michael is what led to the creation of the Facebook group. I think we can all agree we're grateful for that.

Then came the next big question, for individual families and the group at large: What do we do with all of this information about Michael? Is it right to have and share it (with our children or with one another) without his consent? Will it feel like a violation of privacy someday, when the first child reaches out and he realizes we've known his identity all along? Would he have donated at all if he'd understood that the anonymity-until-eighteen rule was an empty promise in a world where anonymity can't be guaranteed?

Some parents chose not to access certain pieces of the available information about Michael, like updated photos or social media handles for a very valid reason: if they didn't have the information, they couldn't be in the position of withholding it from their child. For them, it simply didn't feel ethical to receive it in the first place, given the murkiness of our situation. Melissa and I chose to have the information—all of it.

Once again, this isn't about right or wrong. There's no one-size-fits-all answer. I can believe one thing, and you can believe another, and we can still remain in community with each other. But it does raise a deeper question: What do we owe each other?

We all feel the strangeness of our situation. Our children are genetic relatives, but many of us are still strangers. Do we have new responsibilities simply by becoming part of this group?

One question that inevitably arises is: Is it ethical to have more children using Donor 2XC89 vials or embryos, knowing how many children there are and the problems that can come with large sibling pods? It's an incredibly emotional question, and one I've considered a lot privately as someone who still hopes to have another child using 2XC89 vials.

It begs a broader question: How many families (or donor-conceived offspring) is too many for a single donor? According to our cryobank, there is a "limit" to the number of families our donor can help create. But now that we know these limits are not strictly upheld, we realize the true number of children and families will probably be far larger than we ever could have guessed. Unfortunately, not even the cryobank will know how many donor-conceived siblings there are in the end.

Some donor-conceived people advocate for dramatic reductions, suggesting no more than two families should share a donor. Of course, this would either make sperm donation unprofitable for banks or unaffordable for families, but the benefits to donor-conceived people, donors, and families alike are massive. That kind of shift would require sweeping, systemic change, not just personal sacrifice.

And then, there are moments that make the risks and consequences of our current practices feel terrifyingly real. A recent story broke about donor-conceived children across

Europe who inherited a rare cancer from their genetic father, a sperm donor. At least 65 children were born from that donor, and 10 have been diagnosed with cancer.[xi] The online response was predictable:

"How could they have let this happen?"

"Why were so many children allowed to be born from one donor?"

Those of us inside this system, however, know the truth. This is not an outlier; this is the norm. And more horrifyingly, we realize this could have easily been our children. When I had read that our donor was a carrier for a genetic condition, it was oddly reassuring in a way. It felt like we were able to dodge whatever harmful genes any of us might have passed on (because Melissa and I did genetic screenings as well). Of course, I know better now. I know that the cryobank screenings are far from comprehensive and that a lot can be missed.

So, of course we ask: Is it right to add more children to our already-large pod? There's no correct answer. Each person, each family, has to wrestle with that decision on their own. But even if the choice is personal, the consequences are not. Our decisions ripple outward. How much do we owe the other families, the other children, in our own family-making choices?

My personal belief, in this particular scenario, is that none of us are individually responsible for mending the failings of our cryobank or the fertility industry at large. If there's a certain number of children that tips the scale from ethical to unethical, then: 1) We've already surpassed it, and 2) We've essentially created a race where families who conceive fastest win and those who take longer lose. That would unfairly penalize people with more complex or extended fertility journeys, and it would suggest that some families deserve children more than others.

None of us has more of a right to parenthood than anyone else.

That doesn't make the ethical tension easier to live with.

If we do have another child, Melissa and I believe it would be better for our family to use the 2XC89 vials that we have in storage than to start over with a different donor. I believe it would be better for my son to share a genetic connection with his sibling. I believe it would strengthen our family's ability to engage with the donor-conceived sibling pod. I believe it would make things logistically and emotionally smoother if my children were able to walk one shared path, instead of two parallel ones. Could that be seen as a selfish choice, when we could also choose to not have another child at all? Absolutely. If you disagree, I fully respect that. Feel free to make a different choice for your own family.

I don't take this lightly. I know that my actions have weight. A genetic sibling for my son would also be a genetic sibling for more than 40 other kids. What is best for us might not necessarily be best for them. And I remember frequently that our pod is even larger than it seems.

So, what do we owe each other?

I don't have a definitive answer. But I do have hopes.

I hope we can keep having honest conversations. I hope we can continue to respect our differences and face hard things together. There are no clear answers here, but mutual respect and transparency are essential if we want this community to remain a healthy space for connection. Disagreement is inevitable in such a tender and evolving space, but clarity, honesty, and communication can soften the edges.

The best we can do is move forward with care, openness, and respect for the children at the heart of all this while acknowledging the ambiguity that's part of being a recipient parent and/or donor-conceived person.

CHAPTER NINE

HOW DO WE TALK ABOUT HIM?

After the big emotional conversations with the group subsided, we were each left to reckon with what it all meant in the relative quiet of our own families. Although Melissa and I had now known Michael's identity and been looking at the updated photos for a few months, we hadn't yet updated our donor book for Riley with new photos or Michael's name. We still weren't sure what felt right: what language to use, what tone to set, or what information to include.

When I first made the book, my goal was simple: to share the information we had from the cryobank in a way that felt accessible and age-appropriate. That's still my hope, but I also know the book will continue to evolve as Riley grows—and especially as he begins to express his own language preferences and interest level.

This second time around, we had so much more content to put into the book—not only more humanizing information about Michael, like his name, but more insight from listening to donor-conceived people talk about what has felt meaningful, what language they prefer, and what pitfalls to avoid.

The final pushes that helped me bridge the gap between version one and version two were continued one-on-one conversations with my fellow podparents (parents of Riley's half-siblings) who were approaching things similarly to us.

One of the other NYC parents showed me her own gorgeous version of the book. She helped me realize something I hadn't seen before: in my effort to validate Riley's biological story, I had forgotten myself. I'd forgotten momentarily that while I'm not biologically connected to Riley via ovum or pregnancy, I am still a huge part of how he came to be. I had overcorrected without even meaning to.

Their version gave me some beautiful examples of how the non-genetic parent can (and should) be incorporated into the story. It was also validating in a way I hadn't expected. It was her daughter who originally pointed out the absence of her other mom in the book. Kids notice.

That feeling was reinforced by something I heard in an interview on another donor conception podcast called *Three Makes Baby*:

> "So, if my grandmother had never come over from Germany and moved to New York and had my dad in 1939, and then my dad grew up and had never had a blind date with my mom, who lived in New York, they would never have got married. And then my dad couldn't have kids, so they needed to use a donor. If that had never happened, my mom would have married somebody else and would have had, probably didn't need a donor, and would have moved on with her life.
>
> My dad and my grandma, they absolutely had to live, and they had to be so that I could be. So they are 100% part of my family tree. Without that, I wouldn't be here, even though they're not biologically related to me."[xii]

I didn't realize how deeply I needed the reminder of my importance to Riley. In our day-to-day life I never questioned it, but when it came to this process, I had unconsciously minimized my role.

We rewrote the book to include how Mommy and I chose our sperm donor together. We also added that in addition to needing eggs, sperm and a safe place to grow, children need people to love and care for them once they are born.

Jocelyn helped me reconsider something else. In version one, I had written that Riley might be able to meet Michael one day if he wanted. I had chosen the word *might* carefully, knowing there are no guarantees. But she pointed out that even as written, the sentence could still create unrealistic expectations. Identity disclosure isn't a promise of future connection, much less a meeting, no matter how much I wish it were. I realized including that possibility in the book reflected more of my own hopes than what's actually realistic, especially given the size of our pod. The sentence became, "We might be able to learn more from Michael one day if you want."

There are so many things I'm grateful for when it comes to our sibling pod, but being able to have these conversations together, with specificity and care, is at the top of the list. Parenthood, especially non-traditional parenthood, can be deeply isolating. Walking through this emotional terrain hand-in-hand with others has been one of the most educational and meaningful experiences of my life.

I was surprised by some of the pitfalls I uncovered in my rabid consumption of donor-conceived stories. These stories helped me realize that, in addition to being intentional about language, we also needed to make sure we were setting realistic expectations around who Michael is. It's incredibly tempting to tell a story that casts him as someone altruistic, who donated out of kindness to help families like ours have kids. While that may be part of what happened, there's also a financial incentive that cannot be ignored.

One story I heard from a donor-conceived person on a

podcast stuck with me: when she met her biological father, he was honest about the fact that he had donated sperm, at least partially, for financial gain.[xiii] This affirms my desire to avoid fairytales or convenient white lies to concoct a comfortable, charitable narrative of donor-conception. If a DCP always knows that there could be myriad motivations for someone to donate their genetic material, the truth will not come as a shock or disappointment.

Other stories were more cautionary. Some donor-conceived people have discovered that their parents' donors hold views fundamentally at odds with the families the donors helped create, including homophobia and/or transphobia. Imagine realizing your biological parent disapproves of your family's very existence. While I'd like to believe that cryobanks today are more transparent with their donors about the kinds of families they might help build, especially given that LGBTQ+ people make up an estimated 40-60% of their clientele (though real statistics are hard to come by, which is another issue entirely), these stories reveal just how little recipient parents really know about who their donors are.

Our cryobank shared some information that gave insight into Michael's motivations, but I'm keenly aware there's a marketing spin behind everything they do. While I'm grateful to have this information to pass on to Riley, I also know that people change, and what we've been told is only part of the story.

There are stories of donors marketing themselves to cryobanks in their questionnaire answers, too—they want to be chosen, after all. In Donor Dylan's *Insemination* podcast episode, he recalls how donating sperm was a common stream of income for colleagues in his college fraternity. They shared information with one another about their experiences so they could help their bros get "chosen" too, whether what they told the banks was true or not. Again, finances often win over ethics on many levels.

As a recipient parent, it's tempting to paint a rosy picture of sperm donation. For us, it was obviously about love, family, and possibility. But for donors, the motivations can be more complicated, and for cryobanks they are almost always financial. These are for-profit companies, which I continue to remind myself. As more stories emerge, it's becoming harder to ignore the ways profit continues to distort accountability.

One particularly chilling example came out at an industry conference recently as reported by Laura High from *Insemination* and *LGBTQ Nation*: Seattle Sperm Bank reportedly sold unused vials of donor sperm to the FBI (likely without the donors' knowledge or consent).[xiv] The reasoning remains unclear. The sheer fact that this could happen in secret, though, says everything. It's just one of many examples that reveal how the reality of sperm donation is far more ethically murky than the carefully curated version we're sold. If vials can be sold to government agencies without consent, what else can happen behind the scenes? It's a stark reminder that once gametes leave our bodies, they are at the whims of a system driven by profit, not principle.

Riley is still so young, but the reason I've been working through all this emotional terrain now is so I can practice. This way, I can get comfortable with the language, navigate the nuance, and build a foundation. I want to be ready when he is. I want to model these conversations for him and show him how he might tell his story. If I can speak about his family and his origins with clarity and ease, maybe he'll feel like he can too.

Intentional word choice is a huge part of storytelling, and language in this space is complex. Words carry multiple meanings, but social context shapes how they're received, and our kids don't yet have much context for their situations. Take the word "dad" for example. Is it appropriate to use that word when referring to Michael?

My answer is yes and no. No, because relationships are reciprocal, and it wouldn't be appropriate to imply that if Riley ever met Michael, he could walk up and say, "Hi Dad, it's nice to meet you." But also yes, in the sense that I want Riley to feel permission to use the word (or move past it) without having to launch into a full semantics lesson every time.

"Who is your dad?"

"Why don't you have a dad?"

"Everyone has a dad."

You might think, well, kids don't understand. But questions like these can shape identity. They can chip away at confidence or help build it. And it's not just kids who use the word dad casually. Think about how people talk about DNA surprises. You've probably heard it yourself:

"I found out my dad wasn't my real dad."

Don't even get me started on *real* dad.

Anyway, I digress. Dad can mean both: the person who raised you and the person whose sperm helped conceive you. It can mean neither or something in between. That complexity is part of the story too. Here are some ways I imagine these conversations could play out for Riley:

Q: "Where's your dad?"

A: "My dad was a sperm donor. I have a mommy and an Eba."

Q: "Why don't you have a dad?"

A: "Families can look lots of different ways."

Q: "Everyone has a dad."

A: "Not everyone has a dad in their family. My bio dad was a sperm donor."

For most young kids, "dad" means both the person whose sperm helped make a child and the man raising them. That's what they see and how most families around them are shaped. How would they know anything else? Unfortunately, in many social situations Riley will be the one who has to introduce the idea that families can look different and that dad can mean more than one thing.

I have spent a lot of time reflecting on my own conversations with peers at a young age, and I've realized how often biological connection came up casually in my peer circles and pop culture. For example, I can't tell you how many times I was part of a conversation that began something like: "Do you look more like your mom or your dad?"

These kinds of questions are a very normal part of early identity formation, and that's why I don't think we should reject the word "dad" entirely. I want Riley to feel confident talking about his story, not burdened by it. If using "dad" helps him communicate in a world that still sees family in narrow terms, I don't have a problem with him using it. The deeper context will come with time, experience, and with us continuing to set expectations and having these conversations as a family. Of course, at this point it's all hypothetical. I understand that our language and approach will change as we go.

I've had a lot of practice talking to young children about

identities that adults can struggle to understand. My gender identity is one such example. At our family daycare, I changed from Ms. Lilly to Mx. Eli (Mx. is pronounced "mix") and began using they/them pronouns. It was the last place in my life where I made the switch. I'd already been out as Eli socially for two years at that point. Coming out at work was the final piece of the puzzle before I was my true self in every space in my life. I was so nervous at first, mostly because I was unsure how the families and children would react or how to have those conversations in an age-appropriate way, but luckily it turned out to be much easier than I'd imagined.

> Pre-schooler: "Are you a boy or a girl?"
>
> Me: "I'm kind of like a boy and kind of like a girl."
>
> Pre-schooler: "Oh, okay. Want to play blocks with me?"

Or another of my favorite examples:

> Pre-schooler: "Why are you wearing a tie? Ties are for boys."
>
> Me: "Wearing a tie makes me happy! What kind of clothes make you happy?"
>
> Pre-schooler: "I love sparkly dresses!"
>
> Me: "I love your sparkly dress! I get to choose what I wear, so I wear whatever makes me feel good, like ties. Do sparkly dresses make you feel good?"

That's the kind of ease and flexibility I want to bring to these conversations with Riley. That same adaptability applies to so many other words in our world: family, parent, sibling, brother, sister, mom, dad. Some people ask, "If you call these same-donor-conceived kids 'siblings', does that take something away from the siblings in your own family? From 'full' siblings?" Of course not. Language doesn't need to be gatekept to hold meaning. Let it stretch. Let it affirm. I believe people should use whatever language feels most true to them. But I also believe we can't tell others *not* to use language that reflects biological reality.

Unfortunately, adults have always been more difficult than children when it comes to allowing for this kind of flexibility in language (and in thought). Our own conversations, both within our pod and outside of it, have given us insight into the wide range of reactions people might have when Riley shares his story one day.

One of our goals has always been to help the people closest to us understand our language choices and intentions when it comes to Riley. We don't want them to be caught off guard or put in a position where they don't know how to respond if he brings something up. For us, it's both an opportunity to educate and a way to prepare our community to better support Riley as he grows.

In doing so, we've encountered all kinds of reactions, just like we have in our sibling pod. The main difference is that this world is really hard to grasp unless you're living inside of it. Some people don't understand why we'd want to connect with the other families, much less spend time and energy building real relationships with them. They see it as optional, maybe even cute or a little odd. But to us, it's foundational.

Others struggle with the idea that someone would breach a cryobank's anonymity policy to learn more about their donor. It's easy for people to identify with Michael, an adult whose privacy has been infringed upon. It is not easy for people to identify with Riley, a donor-conceived child with a right to know about his biological relatives. The ethics of privacy can seem clear-cut from the outside, but once you hear enough donor-conceived voices, and once you understand how the industry actually operates, that frame of reference shifts. Most people in our lives haven't had access to that knowledge. I don't fault them for it, of course, but I do have to remind myself that their starting point is different from mine.

What's been most interesting, though, is how often people try to reassure me by minimizing Michael's role. They're quick to remind me that I'm Riley's *real* parent. That the donor was "just" a donor. That he's not important, or not someone worth talking about or focusing on. I understand their impulses. They want to affirm me. But what they don't see is that those comments erase the real complexity. They reflect a world that still doesn't know how to hold nuance when it comes to family, biology, and belonging.

That's why my fellow podparents remain such a lifeline. They're the only ones who truly get it. The only ones who understand the weight, the joy, the weirdness, the wonder. The only ones who don't need a primer before we start the conversation.

So, I'm glad to be having those conversations now, while Riley is young. We're fielding the questions, holding the confusion, making space for it all so that he doesn't have to (at least not as much). That way, if Riley one day says, "My dad's name is Michael," it doesn't stop someone dead in their tracks. It won't be a moment of shock or disbelief. Ideally, it will just be another part of who he is—something his people outside of the pod already understand.

By the time we reached the end of this process, we didn't just have a new version of our donor book with more nuance, more humanity, and more of me. We had something deeper: a clear and intentional understanding of how we want to model conversations about our family for Riley.

Our hope is to give him tools and permission to tell his story however he wants to. To hear his story told with nuance and complexity from the start, and in ways that grow with him. To have parents who show, not just say, that we're safe people to ask questions of. That we are allies in his self-understanding.

That we love every part of what makes him who he is.

Eli Ramos

CHAPTER TEN

OUR LARGE AND GROWING FAMILY

Our Facebook group now includes over 30 families and 40 children across three countries. We've met over a dozen of my son's siblings in person and have developed close relationships with quite a few of the families. Over the last winter, we gathered with the other NYC families every month. Our children attended each other's birthday parties, and we even went on a double date with one of the other NYC couples, kid free!

Among the families we haven't met in person, including most of the international ones, we've video chatted with many. My son loves looking through his sibling book, getting especially excited at every page that mentions vehicles (a common love among many of the siblings).

As parents, we've built meaningful relationships as well. Jocelyn and I now text daily, sharing pictures of our kids, talking about donor conception, and simply becoming good friends. Our kids have even become pen pals, sending each other letters, stickers, and little things in the mail. It's strange to think we've never met in real life, considering how deeply she knows me. She's in this with me. She has become so integral to my journey, and to my understanding of donor conception, in ways that have completely surprised me. Our families don't approach everything the exact same way, but we're both better for having explored our values and hopes together, openly and without judgment.

Melissa and I have become close with many of the other parents too. While we can't all message with the same frequency, especially factoring in different time zones and the varying ages and needs of our children, we connect regularly with many of them. Personally, as one of the parents who has been to a large gathering, who helped put together the sibling book, and who helped facilitate the conversation around the donor's identity, I've had the privilege of getting to know many families more intimately. I consider myself extremely lucky.

We are gearing up for this year's gathering, where more than a dozen families will be convening in Pennsylvania. We will be meeting five of Riley's siblings for the very first time. It'll be our biggest gathering yet, and our first since Michael's identity became known widely within the group.

In many ways, we're still settling from the Michael bombshell and the emotionally complicated conversations that followed. Some parents are less inclined to share openly in the bigger group now, which I understand. Trust is being rebuilt. As our group grows, the inevitability of cliques and side groups forming has begun to show. Naturally, we've grown closest to the other NYC families because we see them the most. Our children have developed real friendships through playdates and shared local adventures, like an afternoon at the Central Park Zoo or Queens Agricultural Fair.

And then, there are other parents I've hardly spoken to yet. Maybe one day we will.

Another complicating issue within our pod is family planning. Some families have posted in the group hoping to have another 2XC89 child, asking if anyone has vials to sell because there are no more available through the bank. Michael has no vial availability on the website, is no longer donating, and is now listed as a sibling-only donor. That means that if any vials were to become available (if a family sells unused vials back to the bank), they're reserved solely for purchase by families who already have a Donor 2XC89 child.

I have complicated feelings about all of this. As you know, we have a few vials stored, hoping we might one day try for another child. But we don't know if that's something we'll be able to pursue. And yet, holding onto vials for a "maybe" feels selfish when other families are at a clear "yes." I feel guilty. I wish we had certainty about whether we'll try again and how many vials we'd need if we did. But we don't.

We've made the choice that if we decide not to try again, or if we don't need all of our vials, we'll give them to other families in the pod. That feels right for us. But even that gets complicated. How would we choose who gets them? I understand why someone might prefer to sell their vials back to the bank (if it's an option) or to no one at all, removing themselves from the emotional calculus of picking one family over another. Once again, we'll cross that bridge when we get to it. Right now, all we have are hopes, not a plan.

I'm grateful these conversations are happening within the pod. I know of families who've offered vials to others when they ran out. Jocelyn even had another family step in and offer a vial when her own shipment was damaged in transit (a nightmare I hope never to experience). It makes me feel better knowing that additional 2XC89 kids are coming into the world through families already connected to our group, rather than from entirely new families starting from scratch. The cryobank enforces this sibling-only policy, but unfortunately, there are still loopholes, and a terrifying gray market.

If a family has leftover vials (that can't be sold back) or frozen embryos, they face a wide range of choices. Some destroy them. Some donate embryos to science. But others may choose to donate embryos or gametes to other families, whether that's now or a decade from now. The cryobank wouldn't know. I have watched sperm vials end up for sale via private exchanges on Reddit. I've seen people post in queer parenting forums, offering extra vials directly to other individuals.

While I'm reassured by the actions I've seen within our own pod, people acting thoughtfully and with care, I don't know how many other 2XC89 families are out there or what decisions they might make with their own additional sperm vials or embryos. Their choices could ripple through all our lives.

These issues are not unknown to cryobanks. How do I know? There are a few cryobanks now that offer more exclusive options for families. For sometimes more than twice the price, families can purchase sperm from a donor who is shared with fewer families…a smaller family limit. What the fuck?

This shows, very clearly, that cryobanks understand the appeal of smaller family limits. They know the risks of anonymity, over distribution, and the emotional impact of sprawling sibling networks. But instead of implementing ethical limits across the board, they're monetizing the very scarcity they helped create.

Re-reading cryobank policies now, I am shocked at how non-committal the language is around family limits. The veil has been lifted.

California Cryobank Website:

"Our maximum goal is 25-30 family units worldwide per donor."[xv]

I have to call out the wording "maximum goal". What does that even mean?

Seattle Sperm Bank FAQs:

> "We have a 25 family limit nationwide for our donors. This is monitored by our Pregnancy and Birth Reporting, which is a requirement for all purchasers.
>
> Pregnancy and Birth reports can be submitted to us at this link:"[xvi]

As of this moment (July 7th, 2025), there is no link following the colon on this page of their website (not on mobile or desktop).

Fairfax Cryobank Website:

> "We consider a family to be created when a person or couple has a child using one of our donors. Once 25 individual families have been reported in the US, we stop distributing the donor's vials to new clients in the US.
>
> Once 15 families have been reported outside the US, we stop distributing the donor's vials to new clients outside the US."[xvii]

The key phrase here is "once families have been reported." There's no real data about how many don't report. The second issue is that defining family as when someone has a child means that 25 families could be reported, they could stop selling sperm, but an unknown number of families could be pregnant already by the same donor or have their vials or embryos still frozen for a later date.

Cryos International Website:

> "Every country has its own regulations regarding sperm donation and the number of families or women a donor can help."[xviii]

This tells me nothing, as a prospective parent, about how many children may be born from one donor from this bank.

Again, and again, and again, it's not about ethics. It's about profit. Oh, the joys of capitalism.

The profit-driven cryobank model is one of the reasons some families turn to less regulated marketplaces like social media in their search for donor gametes. The realities of these lesser-known family building channels became shockingly clear after the release of *Spermworld*, a documentary about online forums (mainly Facebook) where sperm donors and hopeful parents find one another.

Through online forums like Facebook, families can find a sperm donor. How easy or complicated that search is depends on what they're looking for. Some are intentional, hoping to create a more thoughtful, transparent arrangement with a donor than what cryobanks offer. Some turn to these channels because they cannot find a donor that matches their partner's or their own racial background through a cryobank. Others are there because it is more accessible. Then there are those who are far less selective, posting their location and ovulation dates, inviting any donors who happen to be nearby.

The risks in these channels are vast. Again, there's no regulation regarding how many children one donor can conceive in the US, leading to the issue of serial sperm donors and unchecked offspring numbers. Donor-conceived people often face challenges in understanding their identity, accessing biological family medical history, or connecting with siblings as it is; these issues only deepen when there are no records to begin with.

Then there are the health risks. In some cases, recipients may have little to no information about the donor's medical background. The idea that "love makes a family" can be powerful, but when it's used to minimize the role of donors entirely, or sidestep safety and ethics, it becomes more than dismissive. It becomes dangerous.

There's also a deeply unsettling subset of these arrangements, ones where donors suggest (or push for) "natural insemination," a euphemism for sex. Too many of these informal donors insist on it. It's hard not to see this for what it often is: coercive, exploitative, and just plain predatory. Add to that the legal complications when you conceive informally with a "donor" in this way. Many families enter into these agreements with no legal protections in place. There have been custody battles with donors who later decide they want involvement. Too many children are caught in the legal gray areas of parenthood.

This is the Wild West—not just of conception but of responsibility.

Then there are the serial sperm donors with racist intentions (yes, of course they're white).

There's no question that cost is a major factor leading people to these unregulated channels. Cryobanks are prohibitively expensive for many families, especially queer couples, single parents by choice, or people already navigating financial strain from fertility treatments or systematic disenfranchisement. But in cases where cost becomes the primary concern, structure and accountability often fall away.

So, what gets lost in that tradeoff?

For one, clarity. Without contracts, record keeping, or donor-screening, families risk losing access to critical medical history, semi-accurate sibling counts, and any reliable pathway for the donor-conceived child to learn about their origins should they want to. These children inherit not just the biology but the uncertainty.

What's also lost is the foundation for long-term boundaries and relationships. With no legal safeguards in place, families and donors can find themselves in murky waters navigating unwanted contact, custody disputes, or total absence when a child begins asking questions.

There's also a broader loss: the opportunity to treat donor conception with the intentionality it deserves. When it's treated as a quick, low-cost exchange, the humanity of everyone involved—the donor, the parents, and especially the child— becomes diminished. Structure doesn't mean rigidity; it means respect. It means creating something sustainable, ethical, and transparent. It means considering not just how a child is conceived but how they'll grow up.

Cost matters. But so does what we're building and who we're building it for.

There are new, more ethical ways of family building that are becoming more popular. More donor-conceived people are advocating for known donor arrangements, especially one where a family member or close friend could act as a donor (like the arrangement we had considered). Then there are new services like Seed Scout, that connect families trying to conceive with donors who agree to a different kind of arrangement where they're known from the very beginning. This option, however, is even more cost prohibitive than traditional cryobanks.

In the meantime, Melissa and I must reckon with the circumstances we're already living in. We are part of a large and growing sibling pod. Many of us parents feel a low-level hum of unease, wondering when the next new family will reach out on the DSR or join the Facebook group—and what it will mean when they do.

Adult donor-conceived people sometimes joke that January and February are "sibling season," AKA the months when test results roll in from DNA kits received as holiday gifts. Some people discover unexpectedly, as a result of these seemingly harmless gifts, that they are donor-conceived and have half-siblings in the world. For us though, there is no season. New families can surface at any time, from anywhere.

I've heard from many adult donor-conceived people who say they wish they'd known their half-siblings sooner. They say that those early years of potential connection feel like something lost. That sense was only reaffirmed when I watched *Future People: The Family of Donor 5114*, a documentary following a growing pod of donor siblings and their families. When a new sibling joins partway through, he shares that same aching desire that he had known them earlier and that there had been less mystery. One of my fellow podparents said it best: it's easier for our kids to opt out of this group one day than to opt in without having been a part of it from the start.

For the children in the Donor 5114 documentary, knowing their siblings wasn't universally joyful. Just like in our own community, more people meant more complexity. There was palpable sadness around a lot of their experiences—not knowing how many siblings there were, not having a photo of their biological father, not knowing if he would be open to connecting with them.

There was also a particular burden on the oldest sibling in the group. When she turned 18 and had the opportunity to reach out, the first out of all of the siblings, there was immense pressure on her. All of her siblings waited with bated breath for her birthday to arrive. Her outreach message would be all of theirs. Her own hopes were reflected by so many others. The pressure is unimaginable.

Some parents prefer to wait for their children to express interest one way or another before seeking donor-conceived siblings, but I don't think children know how to ask for something as fundamental as the chance to grow up in connection with their biological kin. Melissa and I want those relationships to be part of Riley's normal life, not a revelation some years down the line. We know these connections won't be without challenges, but neither would their absence. At least with connection, we get the chance to navigate it together.

I also know that not everyone agrees. Some of the families who share our donor, known and unknown to us, are making other choices and I respect that. Some have chosen to connect but not meet in person. Some have chosen not to connect at all. Some may still be on their fertility journey, still trying to conceive with Donor 2XC89, because having a child can be a many yearslong process and sperm can be frozen indefinitely. We may continue to discover newly-born siblings for years, decades even, given the longevity of cryopreserved sperm and embryos.

Each time someone new joins our group, we will have to reorient. It's not easy to step into a space that already has shared history and an established culture, and it's not easy for the rest of us to pause, make room, and begin again. But we'll have to keep doing it over and over again. We'll return to the same difficult conversations because this is the choice we have made and the situation we have found ourselves in.

Some of the newest members of our crew are younger siblings in families already within the group, like Otto's new adorable little brother. We are still sharing pregnancy and birth announcements and supporting one another privately in our fertility and family building journeys. While some families may be done having children, others are actively trying for more. It's a strange contradiction feeling overwhelmed by the size of our pod while also being thrilled when someone has the family they've hoped for. The number feels abstract, but each new child is a living, breathing dream come true.

Through all of it, the critiques of the industry, the legal gray areas, the complexities of our pod, the unknowables of the future, I keep coming back to care—not institutional policy or abstract ethics but the kind of care we offer each other.

Within our pod, we've built something that doesn't exist in any cryobank's fine print: independent interdependence. No one is obligated to show up, and yet, many of us do. We offer what we can, when we can: hand-me-downs, a listening ear, a group chat that keeps us going through the everyday slog of life with a toddler. Sometimes that care is emotional, sometimes logistical like planning our group trips or housing shared documents. Sometimes it's just presence like a shared meal, a birthday party, a photo of a new tooth, or a sibling hug.

We've also continued to have hard conversations about privacy, language, access, and disclosure. About how our choices might differ and how we navigate those differences while still choosing each other.

This group was never about total agreement. The goal of these challenging conversations has never been to think the same way or parent the same way. The only goal, really, is to keep choosing care over comfort. To stay in the room when things get complicated. To speak honestly and listen generously. That, to me, is ethical practice.

It's also what I hope Riley inherits. Not just the biology that connects him to this group but the culture we're building together. It's one that values transparency, curiosity, and mutual respect. It's one that can hold difference without fracturing. It's one where he sees that family isn't just something you're born into, it's something you can choose—something you can grow, shape, and nurture with intention.

Not everyone would use the word, but I do consider our pod to be family. Not in the traditional sense, but in the way we show up for each other, share burdens, and commit to one another's children. I feel part of something new with all of them. Together, we are tending unique relationships and laying the foundations for a different kind of community rooted in intention and care. We're not ignoring the challenges created by the systems we're part of; we're naming them and asking how to do better.

Our family is still growing.

So is our understanding of what it means to belong to it.

CHAPTER ELEVEN

WHERE DO WE GO FROM HERE?

Our children are growing up in a different world than the donor-conceived people who came before them. Still, we're navigating a broken system rife with personal and ethical uncertainty.

We're living through a pivotal moment in donor conception, finally asking the questions that should have been central from the start as at-home DNA tests continue to unearth long-held family secrets. Donor-conceived people are speaking out, sharing their stories, and demanding accountability. More families like ours are finding one another. More people are contacting formerly anonymous donors. Some countries have even banned donor anonymity altogether. The landscape is shifting, and I know which direction I hope we're heading.

Our pod is such an interesting organism. It's something I'm incredibly proud to be part of because it has become central to how I understand this world. Within it, I've found incredible allies in many of my fellow podparents—people who are also hoping to build something better for the future. Our children are still so young (all of them are under five) but we're already establishing a foundation that we feel good about and hope will support them as they grow.

As meaningful and (mostly) wonderful as my experience in the pod has been, it's also a constant, sobering reminder of how much change is still needed. The sheer size of our group, the persistent uncertainty about how many families and children actually exist, the unease around Michael's openness and his potential response to our children reaching out someday, and the ongoing harm caused by outdated, defensive, or dismissive industry rhetoric name only a few. There's also a part of me that wonders if any of us will ever run into Michael by accident, or if he will ever reach back out or look for us. I don't know how I'd react or what I'd even want. Even as the pod offers joy, connection, and possibility, it also makes us confront a necessary reckoning.

One of the conversations that's come up in our group, especially since the start of the second Trump administration, is the need for some of us to legally adopt our own children. While straight, cisgender couples who use donor sperm are automatically granted parental rights for both parents, the same isn't true for queer couples like ours. If I were a man, and nothing else changed (same donor, same process) I would be legally recognized as Riley's parent automatically and without question. But because I'm not a man, I had to adopt him (and yes, that was necessary even though I am on his birth certificate).

Not every parent in my position chooses to pursue adoption. For me, it was about safety. Without it, there's legal precedent for all kinds of complications in worst-case scenarios like if Melissa were to die, if we divorced, if there were custody disputes or decisions around medical care. Melissa would never do this to me, but there is a current custody battle where the non-biological mom's lack of DNA connection to her children is being used in an attempt to limit her parental rights. Even something as simple as international travel could become fraught without explicit legal protection. Then there's the everyday possibility of discrimination, of being told, implicitly or explicitly, that I don't count—that I'm not a legitimate parent.

The best part of the process of securing my legal rights was that, thanks to both the state I live in and the support of Otto's parents, the undertaking was made infinitely easier than it might have been. We had all our paperwork completed and a court date set for our hearing before Riley was even born.

Otto's family generously walked us through our options and helped us feel prepared because they had already gone through the process themselves. In New York, there's a more accessible legal pathway called a Judgment and Order of Parentage. Unlike traditional adoption, it doesn't require invasive evaluations of your finances, health, home, or relationship.

I'd read *Confessions of the Other Mother: Non-Biological Lesbian Moms Tell All* edited by Harlyn Aizley before we even conceived, so I had a sense of what full adoption might entail, and I was immeasurably grateful I didn't have to endure the same level of scrutiny that parents in other states did. Not because I doubted my ability to "measure up" but because the process sounds, frankly, humiliating. The fact that straight cisgender families don't have to go through it is not just unfair; it's infuriating.

We had practically zero hoops to jump through to have a child. If we had money, we could buy sperm. But to be legally recognized as our child's parent? That's where the system decides to draw the line? Make it make sense.

And unfortunately, this is just one example in a broader pattern of inequality for LGBTQ+ families. For us, rights depend more on our zip code than on our humanity.

I am very fortunate to live in New York, and I hope other states will one day pass similar legislation to create pathways for queer families.

While queer families fight for the right to be recognized

and protected, we're also relying on, and implicated in, a fertility industry with deep structural flaws. As donor-conceived people and their allies demand long-overdue reform, those of us building families this way need to listen, reflect, and advocate, too. Donor-conceived advocates call for reforms such as: banning anonymous donation, enforcing smaller and truly-capped family limits, requiring donor medical updates, and implementing mandatory birth reporting. They advocate for comprehensive physical and psychological screening, transparency around donor motivations, and guaranteed access to biological origin and health information for offspring. There are growing calls for accountability measures like stricter data reporting by cryobanks and clinics, consequences for mishandled or egregious cases, and regulation of informal donor networks to prevent exploitation and serial donation.

I want to add my voice to those calling for a shift away from the current for-profit, largely unregulated cryobank model and toward one rooted in ethics, transparency, and accountability. I imagine better public education around the risks of unregulated sperm donation, expanded access to affordable and ethical family-building options, and real investment in research on donor-conceived people and their families. I believe we need to center the voices of donor-conceived people in shaping these reforms and that members of the community need to continue sharing their stories. I've learned so much from the voices of donor-conceived people, especially those willing to speak candidly even when the truths are hard to speak. We owe them not just gratitude, but change.

I also believe in building community-based models of care. Our pod, although imperfect, feels like one small example of how care and connection can take root in the cracks of a broken system. It gives me hope for what could come next.

Some opponents of this type of reform would rather prioritize access to fertility assistance for queer people. It is inescapable that some of these advocacy efforts would directly limit family building options for many members of the LGBTQ+ community.

Reform will take time, and equity in access even longer. There is discomfort in the fact that I've benefited from this system, even as I condemn it. That dichotomy is real, but so is the reality that the system was designed to keep people like me in the dark, preying on our vulnerability while charging us for the privilege.

Too often, the people created as a result of these systems, our kids, are the ones that end up shouldering the consequences. I believe they deserve better.

CHAPTER TWELVE

INTO THE UNKNOWN

Much like Michael's cryobank profile, this book captures a moment in time, not the reality of lives that are constantly in motion. Once I finally let it go, it will be a still frame in a much larger film—a complex, evolving story that can't be reduced to a single image. There are so many pieces of this puzzle that didn't fit into my own journey within this space but are integral to the experiences of other recipient parents and donor-conceived people. I look forward to hearing more of their stories.

At the start of this journey, and especially during the unfolding of Michael's identity, the fertility industry and our pod was at the top of my mind. My insatiable thirst for DCP and related stories was consuming for a time, but the truth is that in our daily lives, the issues I've discussed here hardly come up. I'm much more caught up in toddler tantrums, picky eating and potty training. Even more than any of that, I'm encompassed in the everyday joy of being Riley's parent.

These days, Melissa and I talk about Michael with Riley mostly through our donor or sibling book, or when a new sibling is born. We talk about how other families also chose Michael as their donor to help build their family. We continue to honor his role through respectful language and storytelling, but he's more context than main character. He is part of our foundation but not the architecture we live inside every day.

That will likely shift. Riley isn't in school yet. He hasn't faced some of the questions his older siblings have encountered about dads or family trees. As he begins to process things more verbally, I know our conversations will grow and adapt. All the imagined scenarios I've played out in my head like family tree assignments, playground Q&As, or genetics lessons will change depending on his understanding, needs, questions, and preferences.

My goal is to make sure he never has to navigate those moments alone. I want him to always knows I am a safe person to come to, not just because of my words but because of my actions. Melissa and I hope to follow his lead while removing obstacles from his path—to equip him with language, confidence, and a deep sense of belonging and love. We don't need to have all the answers, but we must be a steady, safe place to land when he's seeking them.

I want to model what it looks like to move through uncertainty with integrity, openness, and care. I want to teach Riley to choose difficult conversations and discomfort over silence. And when I inevitably get something wrong, I hope to model humility and repair, too. Unfortunately, we are being presented with many opportunities to model these conversations already—like when our elderly well-meaning neighbor asked us who Riley's mom was. When we answered that we were both his parents, he countered "No, I mean who is *the real* mom."

In an effort to prepare a loving and intentional community for Riley, the closest people in our lives know that Michael's identity has been uncovered and the ways we plan to approach these conversations with him. They've, understandably, had a wide range of reactions to the news. We have shown people his photo and want to make sure we're not the only ones prepared to support Riley with intention in this journey. This book has been a tool for me to understand and organize my thoughts, but it will also be an important method for sharing this world with people outside of it. No one knows what it is like to be a recipient parent until you are one. It's so isolating that, sometimes, I need a neutral ear to help me process it all—someone who doesn't try to solve or simplify. My therapist helps with that, and I encourage others on this path to take their mental health seriously.

Some of my conversations with friends, family and adult donor-conceived people have been difficult. My experiences on this learning journey, and the experiences of those willing to share their own stories, have reminded me of a favorite quote by Stephen King that I found especially meaningful as I was coming out as nonbinary:

> "The most important things are the hardest to say. They are the things you get ashamed of, because words diminish them—words shrink things that seemed limitless when they were in your head to no more than living size when they're brought out. But it's more than that, isn't it? The most important things lie too close to wherever your secret heart is buried, like landmarks to a treasure your enemies would love to steal away. And you may make revelations that cost you dearly only to have people look at you in a funny way, not understanding what you've said at all, or why you thought it was so important that you almost cried while you were saying it. That's the worst, I think. When the secret stays locked within not for want of a teller but for want of an understanding ear."[xix]

I will do what I can to make sure Riley is surrounded with understanding ears, within and outside of the sibling group.

We will continue our relationships within the pod unless Riley chooses to step back from it, which would be his right. Regardless, I will not be stepping back from the relationships I've formed, even if he does. I'm part of this community too. I hope these bonds with other parents who are navigating this new terrain alongside me will remain a vital source of support and reflection for years to come.

I look forward to what's ahead with Riley's siblings: our upcoming gathering, birthdays, shared adventures (including a monster truck show with Otto!), and easy hangs at the park or someone's apartment. Every text or photo from another pod parent still gives me a little jolt of joy. I've loved watching these children grow over the past three years, and it's a pleasure witnessing the ways their families are growing, too.

I hope the shared values that brought us together continue to bind us, even as our choices diverge. I hope we evolve alongside our children. I hope this remains a space we can return to when we need each other most.

I'm not waiting for schools or systems to catch up. We're creating something they haven't made room for yet.

It's a privilege to be part of this pod. It's a privilege to know my son's siblings. But the greatest privilege of all is being Riley's parent.

CHAPTER THIRTEEN

TO MY SON

Dear Riley,

I didn't write this book for you, but I'd understand if you wanted to read it one day. If that day ever comes, I didn't want to miss the chance to speak to you directly.

Although this wasn't written with you as the intended audience, the learning has always been about you. A lot of what's in these pages may never become part of our lived experience, but I still felt it was important to explore and understand this world so that I could be the best parent possible. Doing so has helped me work through some of the emotions that come with being a parent on this path—emotions that too often go unspoken or repressed. I'm glad to have done that work now, because I hope it makes it easier to talk with you about the complexities when the time comes. I wasn't afforded the privilege of honest, difficult conversations when I was a child, and I hated being left in the dark.

My only real hope is to be the best parent I can be and to support you in whatever ways you need as you grow. I know that there's no such thing as a perfect parent, but I'm proud of the choices your mom and I have made to lead with transparency, love, and connection.

The experience of learning from donor-conceived people and organizing my thoughts into this book has been incredibly humbling. A few of the qualities I believe are extremely important in life are curiosity, humility, gratitude and kindness. I know I'll continue to be humbled, both as a person and as your parent. Eventually, I'll be learning more about it all from you, too. I'm forever grateful for you, and I will always treat you with kindness, through this journey and every other.

As cliché as it sounds, you coming into the world is the best thing that has ever happened to me. Being your Eba has brought me more joy than anything else in my life ever has. I am proud of you and proud of our family. I hope you are too.

I love you, no matter who you become. I can't wait to see what life has in store for you and for our family. You are already the best person I know.

Thank you for making me a parent. Loving you is the best thing I've ever done.

With all my love and immense gratitude,

Your Eba

ACKNOWLEDGMENTS

First and foremost, to my wife and child—thank you for being my family. I love you more than anything in this world.

To my editors, formal and informal, thank you for helping this book become what it has.

To my fellow podparents—many of you deserve to be individually named for the ways you've supported me in parenting, in learning, and in making this book. Thank you for your candor and vulnerability. Thank you for digging into the hard stuff with me. Thank you for being my friends. And thank you to the forces that brought us together. This journey is far from easy, but I'm so glad to be walking it alongside you and your beautiful families.

To the donor-conceived people who are sharing their stories, advocating for change, and educating parents like me— thank you. You are doing the real hard work, and your voices are already reshaping the future. I hope more people continue to listen. A special thank you to those who have connected with me personally and encouraged this book into being. Your own writing helped me find my path here.

To our extended family and friends—thank you for loving us and supporting us as we build a family on our own terms. We love our life because of you.

And to our donor—words fall short. Whatever your journey in this space may be, your donation helped create the brightest chapter of our lives. Parenthood is the greatest gift, and we have you to thank for making it possible. We hold that with deep and abiding gratitude.

ABOUT THE AUTHOR

Eli Ramos is a queer, nonbinary parent, educator, and community builder. They live in New York City with their wife and son. Eli was driven to write this book after becoming a recipient parent and learning the truth of the complex, largely unregulated world of donor conception.

Their writing explores themes of identity, family, and parenting with intention. *My Son's Siblings* is their first book.

Contact: eli.ramos.author@gmail.com

Eli Ramos

REFERENCES

[i] Obergefell v. Hodges, 576 U.S. 644 (2015)

[ii] High, Laura. *Insemination*. 13 Dec. 2023, disc 30. Podcast.

[iii] Tucker, Angela. *"You Should Be Grateful."* Beacon Press, 18 Apr. 2023.

[iv] Musk, Vivian. 2025. "My assigned sex at birth was a commodity that was bought and paid for. So when I was feminine as a child and then turned out to be transgender, I was going against the product that was sold." Threads, March, 10, 2025, https://www.threads.com/@vivllainous

[v] High, Laura. *Insemination*. 13 Dec. 2023, disc 30. Podcast.

[vi] *Assisted Reproductive Treatment Amendment Act 2016* (Vic) No 6. https://www.legislation.vic.gov.au/as-made/acts/assisted-reproductive-treatment-amendment-act-2016.

[vii] ---. "A Brief History of Donor Conception." *HuffPost*, HuffPost, 10 May 2016, www.huffpost.com/entry/a-brief-history-of-donor-conception_b_9814184

[viii] Ludwig, Nick. *Inconceivably Connected*. 30 June 2025, disc 1. Podcast.

[ix] "Donor Conceived People Present at the United Nations - We Are Donor Conceived." *We Are Donor Conceived*, 18 Dec. 2019, www.wearedonorconceived.com/guides/donor-conceived-people-present-at-the-united-nations/. Accessed 20 Jul. 2025.

[x] Ludwig, Nick. *Inconceivably Connected*. 30 June 2025, disc 8. Podcast.

[xi] Devlin, Hannah. "Sperm from Cancer-Risk Donor Used to Conceive at Least 67 Children across Europe." *The Guardian*, The Guardian, 23 May 2025, www.theguardian.com/science/2025/may/23/sperm-donor-cancer-risk-children-europe. Accessed 20 Aug. 2025.

[xii] Rupnow, Jana. *Three Makes Baby*. 27 Apr. 2024, disc Lindsay B On same donor siblings, DNA testing your child and more (part 2). Podcast.

[xiii] McLaughlin, Louise. *You Look like Me*. 23 Apr. 2023, disc BONUS EPISODE: Send This To...A Donor. Podcast.

[xiv] Sprayregen, Molly. "Private Sperm Bank Admits to Giving Sperm Samples to FBI without Donors' Knowledge - LGBTQ Nation." *LGBTQ Nation*, 21 May 2025, www.lgbtqnation.com/2025/05/private-sperm-bank-admits-to-giving-sperm-samples-to-fbi-without-donors-knowledge/.

Accessed 20 Jul. 2025.

xv "Frequently Asked Questions | California Cryobank." *Cryobank.com*, 2025, www.cryobank.com/learning-center/frequently-asked-questions/ Accessed 25 Jul. 2025.

xvi "Seattle Sperm Bank - FAQ - Frequently Asked Questions." *Seattle Sperm Bank*, 29 Apr. 2025, www.seattlespermbank.com/faq/ . Accessed 25 Jul. 2025.

xvii "Sperm Sperm Donor Birth Limits | Fairfax Cryobank." *Fairfax Cryobank - Find a Sperm Donor*, 11 Mar. 2025, fairfaxcryobank.com/donor-birth-limits Accessed 25 Jul. 2025.

xviii *Cryosinternational.com*, 2025, www.cryosinternational.com/en-gb/dk-donor/donate-sperm/sperm-donor-faq/sperm-donation-everything-you-need-to-know/how-many-children-can-a-sperm-donor-help-conceive/ Accessed 25 Jul. 2025.